R Guide to Masterpieces of Rome

Texts: *Giovanna Uzzani*

SCALA

TABLE OF CONTENTS

Introduction

«Rome should be seen as one city succeeding another, and not simply in terms of the new following the antique, but also the constant succession of different epochs of new and old». Such were the words, in 1786, of the illustrious tourist Johann Wolfang Goethe. He had realised that the full appreciation of each period of figurative culture depended on the preceding one being taken into consideration, right back to remote times. Rome, which can be endlessly decoded, has a leitmotif which runs through and connects everything: the antique. Classicism in all its forms is a constant point of reference in Roman figurative culture. There are some areas of Rome where time seems to stand still and one can walk or stand in admiration in front of antique monuments or ruins which are still impressive, trying to conjure up the past. In the extraordinary continuity of life in the «eternal city», the passing of the centuries and the succession of events and peoples have transformed the urban space. Some antique constructions can be seen as they once were, although sometimes their significance has been misunderstood or changed for long periods of time, as in the case of temples transformed into Christian churches. Other buildings have been abandoned and, in the course of time, buried under accumulated layers, until being brought to light by excavations, carried out either on the evidence contained in antique sources or simply through maintenance works or whilst

Facing page: detail of the Trevi Fountain

Caravaggio, *Calling of Saint Matthew*, detail. San Luigi dei Francesi

Following pages: panoramic view of Rome

providing the services needed in a modern city. Whole complexes have been intentionally obliterated and covered over in the implementation of new urban plans, or dismantled, from late antiquity onwards, in order to salvage materials, especially precious marbles and metals, which have from time to time served in the building of new architectural jewels like the baroque churches. Lastly, the expanding metropolis has engulfed monuments which were once situated on the edge or beyond the urban modern buildings or immersed in the green of the evocative archeological areas. By visiting the interior of certain single buildings, the entire architectural culture of the city from the Middle Ages to the present day can be visually reconstructed. Thus a medieval bell tower can live side by side with a baroque façade, a stately Renaissance doorway with a lavish rococò balcony, a Roman capital with a classic column. All the same, if one had to sum up the face, style and «form» of modern Rome, one word would suffice: «baroque». Carlo Maderno, Gian Lorenzo Bernini, Francesco Borromini – these are the architects who have changed, turned upside down and reinvented the city's look. With the 17th century urban revival, the square, which had evolved into an open and dynamic space was transformed into a stage of papal power, taking on an aspect which seems completely compatible with the ideology of triumphal catholicism. The baroque square changes the capital's urban structure: a dynamic space which the church façades, palaces and monumental buildings look onto, it becomes a theatre for the ephemeral side of the city. Crowds gather here for solemn religious occasions, theatrical and musical shows and during the investiture of the public and the powerful. The fountains have a specific role in the process of urban change in which the squares became baroque and theatrical, especially those of Gian Lorenzo Bernini. Water, movement, sound and transparency define these «creations of nature», images of vitality and energy. The Barcaccia in Piazza di Spagna, the Fontana del Tritone in Piazza Barberini, the «exhibition» piece for the Aqua Vergine aquaduct and the Fontana dei Quattro Fiumi in Piazza Navona are all emblematic examples. The baroque face of the city lives on as the centuries pass, even when it is tampered with, covered up, disowned: it lived side by side with the new inventions of neoclassical culture in the course of the 18th century, was revived in 19th century bourgeois building and accompanied the solemn rationalism of the 20th century until today it provides inspiration for experimentation in contemporary architecture. the presence of antiquity is also strongly felt in the works of art in the palaces, the churches and the museums of the capital; it is evident in the architecture as well as the succession of styles. Traces of the antique can be glimpsed in medieval fragments, just as the 15th century refined, antiquarian culture left its mark under the frescoes and funerary monuments in the churches and in the heart of pontifical power: the Vatican Palaces. The antique is part and parcel of great Renaissance art, both in the painting of Raphael and the works of Michelangelo, and was fundamental in the decorative renovation of 17th and 18th century churches and houses of the nobility, which today bear the sign, form and image par excellence of Rome. Even Caravaggio, who brought about his realism revolution, still pays homage to antiquity. Neo-classicism, the age of the Grand Tour and then the academic culture of the early 19th century, still regard Rome as the privileged cradle of artistic production. In the shadow of antiquity, and with the benefit of Renaissance texts, artists from all over Europe come here to train and leave their works behind. When the romantic revolution and the collapse of the Pontifical state begin to make Paris and London the preferred goals, Rome loses this centrality but remains a point of reference, an essential yardstick for the Pre-Raphaelites to Art Nouveau, from the monumental arch of the 20 years of fascism to the reactions of 20th century expressionism and abstract art. The only way to find and rediscover the various-sized pieces of Roman art from the Middle Ages to the 20th century is to become immersed in the colour and forms of works kept in the city's churches, which are the true palimpsests of the memory, to scour the annals of the great 17th and 18th century collections in the palaces and villas of the nobility and to tell the stories of the many works kept in the museums. This is how the threads of a unique culture can be drawn together, the unrepeatable heritage of a timeless art.

Renzo Piano, *Auditorium*

Central districts:
Palatine, Esquiline and Oppius Hills

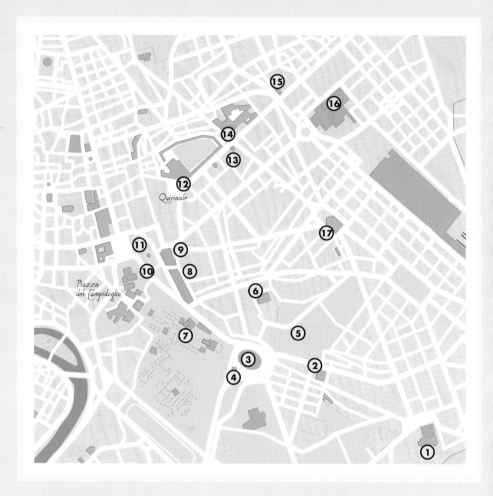

SAN GIOVANNI IN LATERANO

The Lateran cathedral is part of the first monumental complex of the Church of Rome. It was built at the time of Constantine on the site of the ruined home of a powerful Roman family, the Laterani. It consists of a Papal Palace, Basilica and Baptistery, or so-called Patriarchìo, which was used for the diplomatic, residential, defence and administrative purposes of the Pontifical Curia. Until 1300, when Boniface VIII announced the first Jubilee Year, the pontiff resided here with all his dignitaries and the court, enjoying the use of a personal chapel, part of which still exists with the name of Sancta Sanctorum. The building was commissioned by Constantine as a votive offering for the victory over Maxentius, and dedicated to Christ the Saviour in 318 AD. Its blueprint was exactly the same as that of the former Saint Peter's. It must have consisted of a huge space with five aisles divided up by an impressive colonnade. After being damaged several times over the centuries, the Constantine basilica was repeatedly restored until being rebuilt by Francesco Borromini, who gave it its definitive form. In fact the monumental prospect of San Giovani in Laterano is an attempt at combining several architectural languages, with its stately pilasters shielding the five entrance doors which correspond to the five aisles of the basilica. The fifth door on the right, with the cross set in the middle of it, is the Holy Door, which is only opened every twenty-five years on the occasion of the Jubilee. In its spatial proportions the Borrominian cathedral is a faithful copy of the late antique building. In fact it was a condition of the rebuilding commissioned by Pope Innocent on the occasion of the Jubilee in 1650, that the architect Borromini should preserve the original structure of the basilica, saving the wooden ceiling, the five aisle layout and the Martin V Cosmatesque floor.

So Borromini devised a large nave with side openings of five big arches separated by gigantic piers, which comprised the columns of the Constantinian complex. The Piazza San Giovanni in Laterano of today is both one of the richest parts of the city in terms of historical memories, and possibly amongst those most tampered with in the development of the modern city.

A destination for pilgrims and tourists from all over the world, it contains an almost complete synthesis of Roman architectural culture in the form of its monuments, from the Egyptian obelisk to the impressive Imperial age remains, from the Paleo-Christian to the Romanesque, from the late Renaissaince to the Baroque, up to nineteenth and 20th century historicism.

SAN CLEMENTE

In the Basilica of San Clemente, which was built at the beginning of the 12th century, the ancient paintings from the first early Christian basilica have survived and most of the apse and arch mosaics are intact. The main subject of the cycle of frescoes dating back to the end of the 11th century, in the present lower church, is the celebration of the titular saint: the martyr Pope of the primitive church, Clemente. The episodes relating to the life of the saint are portrayed in the nave. The cycle also includes stories from the other saints, including the legend of Saint Alessio.

These frescoes were rediscovered during excavations carried out in the new medieval church, at the end of the 19th century, and constitute important evidence of figurative Roman culture between the 11th and 12th centuries, as well as providing information on the original appearance of the early Christian basilica. The cycle introduces new features in Roman painting at the turn of the 11th century: narrative immediacy, the expressive distortion caused by the emphasis of emotions, and the appearance of naturalistic colouring. On the whole, the frescoes constitute a more sophisticated version of catacomb painting, both in their use of the expressive and

dynamic line and in their revival, in the early Christian sense, of decorative motifs, which are inserted in preordained architectural frameworks. In the bowl-shaped apse there are extraordinarily well-preserved mosaics representing the Cross as Tree of Life, at the top of the hill of Paradise. There are depictions of the doves, symbols of the soul, and, at the base of the Cross, there are two elegant deer drinking from the river and a phoenix, symbols of immortality. The central scene of the Crucifixion combines a more modern, direct and explicit vision with a stately, abstract symbolism. Above the tree, the hand of God the Father is depicted in a star-studded sphere, which is symbolic of the glory of the Lord. In the basilica, in the chapel of Saint Catherine, there is also a fine cycle of Renaissance

frescoes by the painter Masolino da Panicale, portraying *Stories from Saint Catherine and Saint Ambrose*. The pictorial language is based on a knowledge of Brunelleschian perspective but the painting is refined and elegant, thanks to the delicately toned light and a tendency towards a welcome naturalism, as in the tender modelling of the bodies.

Facing page: view of the interior and apse

Masolino da Panicale, *Martyrdom of Saint Catherine*, chapel of Saint Catherine

COLOSSEUM

From the moment it was built, the grandeur of the Flavian Amphitheatre has conditioned Rome's urban landscape and it still dominates the ancient centre. Its arcaded surface was chosen as the theatrical background to the Via dei Fori Imperiali. It was the first amphitheatre to be built in Rome in the form of a monument. In the Republican age the gladiatorial games took place in the Roman Forum, where temporary wooden structures were provided for the occasion. Vespasian, the founder of the Flavian dynasty, emerged victorious from the civil war which followed Nero's death in 69 AD.

As part of a coherent political scheme, the new Emperor decided to dedicate the huge urban spaces and works of art appropriated by Nero to the public, for their enjoyment.

The inhabitants of Rome must have appreciated the building of the big amphitheatre in the centre of the valley, which had previously been the site of the artificial lake made for Nero. The Judaic war, which had ended in 70 AD with the destruction of the temple of Jerusalem, provided the booty and the manpower needed for the construction of the building. It was Vespasian's son, Titus, who inaugurated the amphitheatre in 80 AD, with a memorable gala and games lasting 100 days. The Flavian Amphitheatre was superior in dimensions and monumentality to all those previously built. It was 52 m high, like the northern side near the Via dei Fori Imperiali, which is still intact. The whole of the external wall was faced with marble slabs and decorated with statues in the arcades, and bronze shields hung from the attic storey windows.

The organisation of the internal seating was strictly governed by the laws established by Augustus, through which spectators were seated according to their social class.

The Colosseum was furnished with a sophisticated system of drains which fed the baths and numerous fountains required to keep the vast audience cool. In the amphitheatre there were various kinds of entertainment: fights between pairs of gladiators, hunts involving wild and exotic animals, naval battles and capital punishment executions by exposure to wild beasts, which were also suffered by Christians during periods of persecution. The losers could ask the master of ceremonies, whose decision often depended on the mood of the audience, for mercy. Once the building fell into disuse it gradually deteriorated, and in the Middle Ages dwellings and a fortress were built inside it. The marble facing was systematically removed. Since its rediscovery in the Renaissance, the Colosseum has been one of the monuments which symbolise the grandeur of antique Rome.

ARCH OF CONSTANTINE

The arch, as a type of monument, was well suited to celebrating the ventures and victories, firstly of the consuls in the Republican age and, later on, of the emperors. It was much used in Rome, which is studded with numerous monuments of this type. The arches, which underwent an architectural and stylistic evolution in the course of the centuries, generally either spanned a street or were placed near the entrance of a monumental zone. The bloody civil battle fought on the Milvian Bridge at the gates of Rome on October 28 312 AD, would determine whether Constantine or Maxentius was to have absolute control of the empire. After the victory, and the death of the rival on the battlefield, on the ancient triumphal road in the valley of the Colosseum between the Flavian amphitheatre and the Roman Forum, an honorary arch was erected in honour of Constantine. It is the largest to have survived in Rome, has three arches and is adorned with reliefs and sculptures. The huge monument was the symbolic counterpart of the mere rite of ceremonial entry of the Emperor into Rome. In fact, on the eve of the decisive battle, Constantine had had the famous vision of the cross with the inscription «with this sign you will win», an event which prompted him to place the monogram of Christ on the soldiers' shields and which marked the moment he turned towards Christianity. The Arch of Constantine

is all of 21m high and is built of white marble and articulated in three openings, the middle being the largest. It is flanked by protruding Corinthian columns in antique yellow. Reuse of sculptures or structures from the preceding age was commonplace, and celebratory sculptures were inserted in the arch to enrich the figurative decoration. At the sides of the inscription on the attic storey, there are four rectangular reliefs on each façade, originating from an arch of the Emperor Marcus Aurelius. The eight statues of Dacian prisoners placed in the attic storey against the columns date back to the Trajan age, as do the four stone slabs extracted from a big battle-scene frieze, on the sides of the storey and inside the central arch. Here they are crowned with the inscriptions «to the founder of peace» and «to the liberator of the city», referring to Contantine's victory over Maxentius.

DOMUS AUREA

In 64 BC, a devastating fire, for which the Emperor Nero was not entirely blameless, destroyed most of Rome. The reconstruction of the city encompassed the building of his own residence in the grand style. A huge part of the centre of Rome was transformed into a vast residential area, almost like a city within a city. «A single house took over the Urbs (City)», claims Martial, and Suetonius refers to scornful verses which were displayed around the stunned city: «Rome is turning into a house! Migrate to Veio or Quiriti, provided the house doesn't extend as far as Veio». The residence was planned to occupy an area of between 60 and 80 hectares and extend from the Palatine to the Velia, where the vestibule with the bronze Colossus was, and from the Oppius hill to the valley of the Colosseum and as far as the Coelian hills. The Domus Aurea was not formed of a single palace, but of separate pavillions linked by porticos and terraces and scattered over a

wide area, along the same architectural lines as the villa, which was at that time only found outside Rome. It included cultivated fields, vineyards, meadows, pasture, and woods full of wild as well as tame animals. The building revolved around a series of terraces which rose from the valley with its artificial lake (the future site of the Colosseum) up the slopes of the Oppius. The main body of the complex consisted of five areas radiating from the pivot of the famous Octagonal Hall. These, together with the central nymphaenum, were illuminated by the light which passed firstly through the huge central eye and then through windows cut in the walls below. The marble-clad walls both reflected light and created a sense of lightness. The Octagon may have been the round banqueting hall described in sources, with an ingenious mechanism which revolved day and night, displaying various images. Liberal use of gold-leaf in the frescoes and stucco-work which decorated the interiors was part and parcel of Nero's ideological programme. At the heart of this were worship of the Sun God, with whom the Emperor himself identified, and the launching of a new golden age, from which the name of the residence originated.

MICHELANGELO, *MOSES*
SAN PIETRO IN VINCOLI

The coveted commission of his own splendid mausoleum by Julius II turned into an utter tragedy for Michelangelo, thanks to the continuous interruptions and endless modifications to which the original design was subject. Michelangelo threw himself into the project with great enthusiasm, following the first plan. This envisaged a mausoleum of three storeys decorated with forty statues in marble, and bronze reliefs; the Moses was to form a pendant to the statue of Saint Paul, both being symbols of the mystery of God's revelation. Having spent a considerable time on producing numerous drawings and studies, as well as choosing the marbles in Carrara, the sculptor was forced to abandon the project and concentrate firstly on the work in Saint Peter's, to which Julius II apparently gave precedence, and, after that, on the ceiling of the Sistine Chapel. When the Pope died in 1513, Michelangelo returned to the project, although it had been very much reduced and modified; the mausoleum was no longer free-standing but attached to the walls and it had fewer statues.

The artist undertook to finish this second project within seven years, but, in fact, thirty years would pass before the end product of the tomb in San Pietro in Vincoli was achieved, work on this having only been resumed in 1532 after a long interruption. Between 1513 and 1515 Michelangelo worked on the statues of the first two Prisoners (today in the Louvre), which should have acted as telamons to hold up the architrave beside the two figures of Victories, and that of Moses. The latter undoubtedly represents one of the summits of Michelangelo's art in terms of expressiveness. The rough, nervy quality of the marble surfaces reflects the interior strength, as well as the apprehension, of the prophet of Hebrew law, symbol of the human condition. Hints of antique culture – from the Torso of the Belvedere to the figures of ancient river divinities – blend with echoes from 15th century sculpture, particularly that of Donatello. The figure is seated, the face contracted in concentration and turned towards the left; the right foot rests on the ground, while the left leg is raised with only the point of the foot resting on the base. The biblical figure has a majestic, solemn air in spite of the pervasive feeling of dynamism and withheld energy.

MAXENTIUS BASILICA

The monument, built at the behest of Maxentius in 308 AD, was formerly known as the Basilica Nova or Basilica Costantiniana in reference to the Emperor Constantine, who finished building it. The building was probably the seat of the judicial activity of the praefectus urbi, who controlled the entire judicial and administrative activity of the city from the beginning of the fifth century. In the same period, the seat of the tribunal, where cases concerning senators were heard behind closed doors, was transferred here. Over the centuries the basilica was stripped of its precious elements of architectural furnishing and it is likely that, during the seventh century, Pope Honorius removed the gilded

bronze tiles to use them to cover the roof of Saint Peter's. The ruin of the monument was mainly caused by several earthquakes. The basilica covered most of Velia and a vast portion of the monumental area in the Roman Forum. The choice of the place, which is highly significant in terms of ancient Roman history, was a reflection of deep political and ideological values. Maxentius, carrying on from where his father Maximian Hercules left off, initiated an intense programme of building activity. In terms of the creation of monuments in the grand style, the basilica had an important role in the scheme. The preparation of its site entailed the demolition of the impressive spice store-houses built by Domitian and the removal of another part of the hill of Velia (which had already been modified by Nero for the construction of the Domus Aurea). After the death of Maxentius, who was defeated in 312 AD near the Milvio Bridge, the basilica was perfected by the Emperor Constantine. It has a rectangular plan (100 x 65 m) and was articulated by an ample 35 metre high nave, roofed by three groin vaults resting on eight marble columns, with a large apse at the end. In 1613, Pope Paul V placed the only surviving column in the middle of Piazza Santa Maria Maggiore, where it can still be seen today, forming a base for the statue of the Madonna. Besides the architectural design, the interior furnishings of the basilica were conceived as an expression of the grandiosity of the monument and, at the same time, emphasised the power and magnificence of the Emperor.

IMPERIAL FORUMS

The Imperial Forums were built after Caesar's Forum in Hellenistic style and were conceived as a single architectural project rather than being the result of a series of irregular juxtapositions as in the case of the Roman Forum. The complex owes its monumentality and unique character to its decorative array and the perimeter wall which kept vehicles out. Extensive excavations took place in the Imperial Forums in the 1930s, when the Via dell'Impero, now Via dei Fori Imperiali, was constructed. It was opened in October 1932 as a means of exalting and legitimising the noble Roman origins of the Fascist stock. Other town planning projects were intended to make similar statements, like the monumental opening of the Via della Conciliazione. Today the road still cuts the archeological area in half, concealing important structures, such as the entrance to the Forum of Augustus. Excavations, which were resumed in 1995, were carried out along scientific lines.

The recovery of thousands of square metres of buried sites has made it possible to attain a more perfect reconstruction of the appearance of the monumental centre in the Imperial Age and also to document the subsequent history of the area, which was used for housing in the early Middle Ages.

TRAJAN'S MARKETS

The huge architectural complex of the forum and Trajan's Markets was until late antiquity considered the most famous of Rome's wonders. The impressive project was attributed to Apollodorus of Damascus, a Syrian architect, who worked mainly under the Emperor Trajan, in the first half of the second century AD. This architect, one of the few artists of whom records survive, fused and reworked the fundamental principles of Hellenistic and Roman architecture. The Markets, which were designed at the same time as Trajan's forum, are set on the slopes of the Quirinale, with a series of superimposed terraces. The removal of part of the hill, to a height equivalent to that of Trajan's column, had made space for the creation of a *piazza* (square) in the grand style. The complex, which was designed for commercial and storage use, is articulated on different levels, and its façade consists of a large *exedra* (curving wall), which includes the Forum's eastern side, with eleven *tabernae* (booths) facing it.

The third level consists of a terrace, with more stalls placed along a well-preserved ancient road: the Via Biberatica. This road led to a monumental hall which was the focal point of the complex: it was two storeys high, with a cross-vaulted roof in the grand style and two floors of tabernae. The south side of the hall leads into a series of rooms which were probably dedicated to the administrative offices.

The name Via Biberatica probably originates from the Latin noun *biber* (drink) and may be connected to the trade particular to the booths, possibly taverns, which lined it. The well-preserved road runs straight until it is cut off by the embankment of the modern quarter of Via Quattro Novembre, then follows the curve of the *exedra* in the direction of the Subura, the most famous and infamous popular quarter of Rome, which occupied the valley between the Quirinale and the Esquiline Hill.

There were about a hundred of the small tabernae, partly leaning straight against the rock of the hill. Trajan's Markets were the focal point of the city's commercial activity, with trading taking place within the booths, exactly as in modern commercial centres.

Facing page: view of Via Biberatica

CAESAR'S FORUM

At the end of the first century BC there were so many sacred and civic buildings as well as honorary monuments in the ancient Roman Forum that the area could no longer accommodate the amount of economic, political and judiciary activities carried on in its midst. Julius Caesar was the first to realise the need to expand the city's monument by having another piazza built at his own expense. It was named after him: the Forum Iulium or Caesar's Forum, as it was called in the sources.

The urban project was of fundamental importance to the future history of this area of Rome. In fact it was Caesar (54-46 BC) who chose its significant position near the Republican forum and thus determined the layout of the other four piazzas which were built by successive emperors: the Forum of Augustus (42-2 AD), the Temple of Peace conceived by Vespasiano (71-75 AD), the Forum of Nerva (80-97 AD) and Trajan's Forum (106-112 AD).

These, together with Caesar's Forum, make up the archeological area in the heart of the city, which is nowadays known as the Imperial Forums. In 54 BC, while he was engaged in military campaigns, Caesar entrusted Cicero

and other intermediaries with the task of buying houses and land in the quarter behind the Roman Forum, to build his piazza. A huge sum was spent, between 60 and 100 million sestertius, according to ancient authors.

The complex was inaugurated in 46 BC, to celebrate the triple victory of the leader over Gaul, Egypt and Africa, although Augustus finished it.

The whole of the piazza, which is rectangular in form (160 x 75 m), was uncovered during excavations. It was paved with travertine stone and surrounded on three sides by porticos, dominating the piazza as a focal point in terms of perspective.

Facing page: *The emperor making a sacrifice at the bridge on the Danube,* detail of Trajan's Column

TRAJAN'S COLUMN

The column decorated with historical scenes is a form of monument particular to Rome, and was introduced for the first time in Trajan's forum by the architect Apollodorus of Damascus, who was in charge of the whole project. The reliefs carved on the column are presented in sequence, winding round the shaft up to the top, as a narrative tale, in celebration of the feats and triumphs of the Emperor. The column was dedicated to Trajan in 113 AD by the Senate and the people of Rome, in the forum bearing the same name. The height of the monument (about 40 m) matches the one on the hill, which was dismantled when the complex of the Markets and the Forum was built, as the inscription on the base of the column states. The top of the monument was crowned with a bronze statue of Trajan which has not survived; it was replaced by one of Saint Peter in 1588. The base is in the form

of an altar similar to the funerary altars of the Republican Age, and it served as a tomb for the Emperor; Trajan's ashes were kept in a gold urn placed in the burial chamber inside the base of the column. Here there is a hall leading to a spiral staircase made of marble, with 185 steps leading from the base to the top of the monument.

Termed a cochlite column, like that of Marcus Aurelius, due to the presence of a spiral within the shaft, it was conceived by Trajan's architect, Apollodorus of Damascus. On the outside, the long spiral frieze recounts the two Dacian campaigns with a figure of Victory writing on a shield separating them, but no attempt to create a link between them.

The crossing of the Danube by the Roman army on a bridge of boats marks the beginning of the wars, and there follow battles, sieges, the setting up of encampments, the placing of troops and the submission of the indigenous chiefs to the Emperor.

SANT'ANDREA AL QUIRINALE

With its gilding, marbles, stucco-work and original elliptical layout, Sant'Andrea al Quirinale is one of the masterpieces of sacred Baroque architecture.
On the site of the previous 16th century church, Sant'Andrea a Montecavallo, building started on the new temple for the novitiate of the Jesuits in 1658, at the behest of

Alessandro VII Chigi. Camillo Pamphilj was the patron and Gian Lorenzo Bernini the architect. Construction advanced rapidly and it was completely finished in 1678. It is one of the richest and most harmonious examples of the Baroque architecture of Gian Lorenzo Bernini, and in a very different style from the similar «Borrominian» Baroque masterpiece, San Carlino alle Quattro Fontane. Certain elements are taken from 16th century architecture, but they are given a new slant by Bernini, as in the case of the monumental single tier façade, with its Corinthian pilasters supporting a triangular pediment, which has a large semicircular window in the middle.
The whole gives the impression that the porch resting on ionic columns is upside down. The superb interior, based on that of the Pantheon, has an elliptical plan, with the main axis perpendicular to that of the entrance.
The radial chapels are set back so as not to interrupt the unbroken oval shape, and the impression of spatial airiness is accentuated by the overall diffused luminosity which emanates from the numerous windows in the dome and the lantern.
The light brings out the decorative richness of the interior, with its alternating polychrome marbles, gilding and stucco-work, designed by Bernini himself and executed by Antonio Raggi and others between 1661 and 1666.

Above: vault of the dome

Left: Antonio Raggi,
Saint Andrew in glory

Facing page: façade
of the church

SAN CARLO ALLE QUATTRO FONTANE

For Francesco Borromini, the young architect from Ticino who arrived in Rome in about 1620, the project of the church and convent of San Carlino alle Quattro Fontane, which was commissioned by the Order of the Trinitarians, was decisive, coming as it did after the success of his involvement in Palazzo Barberini. In 1634 Borromini set in motion the building of the convent, which was finished two years later; the church, on the other hand, took longer to complete, as it was begun in 1638 and only finished in 1667. The prospect is animated by an ingenious play of volumes and lines determined by the contrast of concave and convex surfaces. Then there is the elliptical dome with concave niches in the lantern, and, on the left side, the bell tower with its convex belfry and pointed roof. The alternating use of ellipse and oval, concave and convex elements endows the façade with vigour and gives the impression that it is in continuous rotation. The internal space is limited; nonetheless this minuscule, compressed space is the most powerful expression of Borromini's sculptural architecture. The space, which seems minimal at first, teems with the richest and most refined decorations taken from nature: capitals covered in leaves, altar cornices fashioned in the form of bunches of flowers, luxuriant and fleshy friezes of acanthus, culminating in the oval dome. Here the ingeniousness of Borromini makes the structures appear moulded and almost carved, with its unprecedented attention to detail. The refinement and inventiveness is enhanced by the illumination, which is not simply obtained by light filtering from the lantern, but also from little windows placed behind the delicate stucco frieze above the impost of the dome. A tour de force of harmony and proportion, the rooms of the convent are arranged around a cloister where the innovative element of the rounded and slightly convex corners takes the rigidity out of the structures, making them relate to one another in a more articulated and lively way as parts of a whole. The way in which Borromini exploits the linear play in the cornices and the rhythm of the architectural elements in the interests of light is absolutely novel. Simplicity and magic are united in this space, which seems concentrated within a limited circumference. The innovative and ingenious style inaugurated by the works of Borromini had wide-reaching effects throughout Europe and would also have a decisive influence on modern architecture.

PALAZZO BARBERINI

The rise of the Barberini, one of the most powerful of the Roman papal families, is closely connected to the ecclesiastical career of Cardinal Maffeo Barberini, the future Pope, who was elected with the name Urban VIII in 1623. The family's prestige in the papal city was from that moment secured and culminated in the construction in the grand style of the palazzo, which was to become one of the most admired in Rome at the time. Some of the main artists of the age were involved in the building and

decoration of the prestigious residence: Carlo Maderno, Gian Lorenzo Bernini and Francesco Borromini sought to outdo each other in a contest of elegance, as did Pietro da Cortona and Andrea Sacchi in their paintings for the palazzo. Everything, from the architecture to the magnificence of the frescoes and interior furnishings had to reflect the authority and affluence of the line which had chosen this way of leaving an indelible mark on the heart of the city. In 1629, the year in which Maderno died, the palazzo had however only just been begun, so the building was then entrusted to Gian Lorenzo Bernini, the official artist par excellence of the Barberinian court. He saw the construction through, collaborating at first with Francesco Borromini, in whose hands, according to Baldinucci, Maderno had left «the entire care of the palazzo» and who, still in the words of the biographer did «all the designs for the said building». One of the most elaborate residences of Baroque Rome, and a refined theatre for the sumptuous feasts organised by the family, grew from the meeting of these three masters. For instance, on the evening of the 28 February 1656, the Cavallerizza courtyard, on the North side of the building and now part of Via Barberini, was host to a marvellous entertainment given in honour of Cristina of Sweden: a colourful merry-go-round with an elegant parade of carriages and ephemeral displays devised by Giovan Francesco Grimaldi, the family scenographer, and a festive throng drawn from the most prestigious nobility. The reception hall in Palazzo Barberini was decorated between 1633 and 1639 with the splendid fresco painted on the vaulted ceiling by Pietro da Cortona, on an allegorical theme extolling the glory of the papal family and elaborated by the poet Francesco Bracciolini. In the vast hall, which is in fact a huge empty space, the symmetrical forms break away from the traditional system of divisions and frames used by Annibale Carrracci in the Galleria Farnese, to vie with one another in dissolving the boundary between real and painted space in a spectacular new harmony. The impression of magnification is created by the false trabeations framing an open sky. This is animated by scenes symbolising good government and the virtues of the pope and his family. The illusionistic effect is complemented by monochrome clipei at the corners, depicting scenes from Roman history relevant to virtue.

Facing page: palace façade and stairs with Doric columns

Below: spiral staircase

GIAN LORENZO BERNINI, *ECSTASY OF SAINT TERESA*
SANTA MARIA DELLA VITTORIA

In the Cornaro chapel, Bernini accomplished one of his most extraordinary artistic feats, creating a monument which has a remarkable theatrical and illusionistic power. The theme of the chapel was the ecstasy of the Spanish saint, Teresa, who was famed for the unusual spiritual experiences through which she attained mystic union with Christ.

The artist had no trouble portraying the saint in a state of rapture, but the pose is so sensual that the spiritual nature of the event is lost on many observers. It is as if the saint is suspended on a bed of clouds, whose base, because it is darker and placed further back, is at first glance invisible, giving the impression that the marble cloud really is suspended in the air.

However the main theatrical and illusory effect is achieved by the role Bernini so wisely gave to the natural light.

Behind the sculpture he created a small semi-circular apse, which projects from the wall of the church. This enabled him to open a window, which is invisible to people looking at the chapel, at the top of the little apse.

To emphasise the symbolic value of the light, he added a series of gilded rays, which reflect and enhance the light entering through the little window.

The effect was intended to appear supernatural. Bernini had turned the chapel into a theatrical stage with many spectators: the patron, the Venetian cardinal, Federico Cornaro, and his ancestors. In their half-length portraits, they peer from the side boxes as if invited to share in the miraculous event, and seem to cast intent and admiring glances on the drama unfolding on the stage – the central group of the saint with the angel who is about to transfix her with a dart.

In a sense this work is a symbol of the baroque itself: sculpture, light, architecture and painting are fused in a unique tableau of awe and wonder; tangible reality and the illusion of space are indistinguishable and art and imagination are as one.

Left: Gian Lorenzo Bernini, *Cornaro family on the balcony,* Cornaro chapel

MUSEO NAZIONALE ROMANO

The Museum was established in 1889 to house the antiquities of Rome and, not surprisingly, it represents the richest archeological collection in the world. The treasures are displayed in several buildings, including the Palazzo Massimo alle Terme, most of whose grounds were expropriated by the Italian State for the site of the Termini Railway Station. The building was acquired by the State in 1981 and specially adapted to accommodate the museum exhibits. The ground and first floors house a rich collection of sculptures from the Roman era, displayed in chronological order from the Republican Age to the Imperial era, such as the ivory head, the *Girl of Anzio*, the *Crouching Aphrodite* from Villa Adriana, the statue of *Augustus as Pontifex Maximus*, the *Lancellotti Discus Thrower*, and numerous portraits and reliefs. On the second floor precious examples of decorative furnishings are kept, such as the painted garden from the Villa di Livia, frescoes from the Villa Farnesina and the Rome of the Barberini, stucco-work, floor mosaics and the luxurious panels in polychrome marble from the Basilica di Giunio Basso and the

Mithraeum of Santa Prisca. The tour of the museum is rounded off on the ground floor by the important section dedicated to coins and jewels; two items which stand out are the famous gem with the bust of *Athena* and the furnishings for the tomb of Grottarossa, where the mummified body of an eight-year old child was found. The Baths of Diocletian, the largest thermal complex built in Rome, were also chosen to accommodate a museum when the Museo Nazionale Romano was founded. The archeological material is displayed both in the gardens and the Michelangelo cloister of Santa Maria degli Angeli, as well as in rooms inside. The epigraphical section, which enables the history of Latin script to be traced from its first appearance, is one of the most important in existence.

Worth noting among the most significant items are the large clay busts of the goddess *Ceres and her daughter* from Ariccia, and interesting figurative evidence of cults followed in Rome. The first floor of the cloister contains a protohistorical section, illustrating the most ancient phases of life of the Latin peoples, before the rise of Rome, with significant finds originating from recent excavations.

Aphrodite, Roman copy of the original by Doidalsas

Facing page: *Lancellotti Discus Thrower*, Roman copy of the original by Myron

SAINT MARY MAJOR

The basilica built on the northern summit of the Esquiline Hill was originally known as Santa Maria; it was the first basilica in Rome to be named after the Virgin.
In the course of the centuries, with the proliferation of the number of places of worship dedicated to the Madonna in Rome, the name never changed, but the adjective Maior was added in the Carolingian age.
According to legend, Pope Liberius traced the outline of the complex after a miraculous snowfall as long ago as 358 AD. However, it was in the fifth century, with Sixtus III, that the basilica attained the status of the first great building of the Church of Rome, thanks to its guiding role, as well as its central position on the site of the ancient forum and at the point of convergence of main routes.
Its status is justified, given the grand style and opulence of the internal decoration, which was given a didactic role.
The façade was devised by Ferdinando Fuga in about 1743 and articulated in such a way as to incorporate the mosaics of the first façade.
Behind the façade is the soaring bell tower; it is the highest in Rome and, in terms of articulation, it is the last and most monumental in the mould of the Latian

Romanesque prototype.
Five monumental entrances embellished with pillars bearing Corinthian capitals lead to the front portico.
Inside, the nave, whose walls are decorated with the important fifth century mosaic cycle, ends in a monumental Sistine triumphal arch and a 13th century apse. A classical frieze extends right round the basilica under the wooden ceiling.
The iconographic and decorative scheme implemented in the late 16th century by Sixtus V was expressly devoted to the glorification of the figure of the Virgin, whose maternity the Council of Trent had attributed to divinity, contrary to the affirmations of the Protestant Reformation.
The walls of the Sistine Chapel, like the Pauline Chapel in the left aisle, which was designed to house the revered sacred icon of the Madonna, are decorated with a profusion of marbles salvaged from buildings of the Roman era and the former Palazzo Apostolico.

Central districts:
Trevi, Colonna and Campo Marzio

PIAZZA DEL CAMPIDOGLIO

The Piazza del Campidoglio, with the long flight of steps leading up to it, is both the political and physical heart of the city. It was designed in its monumental setting by Michelangelo in 1536, under the patronage of Paul III Farnese. It arguably represents the most perfect translation of the concept of the piazza as an autonomous urban space in 16th century culture. In a masterly reinterpretation of the classic concept of the piazza, Michelangelo reversed the outlook, which had until then been oriented towards the Roman Forum, placing the statue of *Marcus Aurelius* in the middle to face Saint Peter's Basilica. As background, he devised the complete rebuilding of the medieval Palazzo Senatorio, which rose above the ruins of the former Tabularium, and the side wings, made up of the Palazzo dei Conservatori and the Palazzo Nuovo. The latter were completed according to the artist's plans respectively in 1568 and 1655. Uprooted and set obliquely, they endow the piazza with a greater sense of space, and enhance the perspective and theatricality. The geometric star design of the paving, which was implemented in 1940 by Antonio Muñoz based on the plans left by Buonarroti, also emphasises the centrifugal, dynamic dimension of the whole. The robust and imposing plasticity of the architecture adds to the sober stateliness of this area. The façade of Palazzo Senatorio was adapted from

the Michelangelesque plan by Giacomo Della Porta and Girolamo Rainaldi, with its entrance facing the piazza, characteristic double flights of steps, stucco facing and row of gigantic Corinthian pilaster strips. The balustrade looking out over the city, with its monumental *Dioscuri*, was also conceived to complement the piazza, and was modified by Della Porta in 1585.

MUSEI CAPITOLINI

The Capitoline Museum, the oldest museum collection of antiquity, was built at the behest of Pope Sixtus IV, who, in 1471, gave the Roman people four famous bronze statues (the *Capitoline Wolf*, the *Spinario*, the *Camillo* and the *Head of Constantine* with the hand and the globe) which had hitherto been kept in front of the Lateran Patriarchìo as a symbol of the continuity between Imperial Rome and the Church. With the construction of the Palazzo Nuovo, commissioned by Clement VIII in 1603, most of the works hoarded in the Palazzo dei Conservatori could be accommodated. In 1734 the Capitoline Museum was opened to the public after Pope Clement XII arranged for the acquisition of the collection of statues and portraits belonging to Cardinal Albani. In the middle of the 18th century Pope Benedict XIV founded the Pinacoteca Capitolina which was rich in paintings from private collections. After numerous urban excavations organised at the end of 1800 to celebrate Rome as capital city, huge quantities of material flowed in to the museum and new exhibition centres were set up, including the Capitoline Medal Collection. Between 1925 and 1930 the Museo Mussolini, which became the Museo Nuovo, was founded after the acquisition of Palazzo Caffarelli. In 1956 the Palazzo dei Conservatori was enlarged with the construction of the Braccio Nuovo, where important sculptures from Republican Rome were exhibited. Renovation work in the Capitoline Museum has brought about the creation of other decentralised branches. The reorganisation of exhibition space allocated to the Capitoline Museum complex has led to the *Tabularium* being opened to the public.

Above: Caravaggio,
Fortune teller

Left: *Capitoline Wolf*

Right: *Mosaic of the doves*

PIAZZA VENEZIA

In 1466 Paul II moved two huge Terme di Caracalla granite basins from the original platea nova to Piazza Farnese. Thus the reigning pontiff implemented the first phase in the evolution of Piazza Venezia, which, as the monumental figurehead of the Corso, was taking shape in relation to the gradual building of Palazzo Venezia. It represented the first big urban change in Renaissance Rome and became the theatrical arrival point of the famous race of the Bàrberi which, in carnival season, started in Piazza del Popolo and wound its way along the Corso with a festive crowd and the richest nobility looking on. A dense urban network of medieval origin linked it to the Capitoline Hill and an area of crowded fifteenth and sixteenth buildings joined it to the Monti rione beyond the Imperial Forums. When the decision was taken in 1882 to erect the monument to Vittorio Emanuele II as a backdrop to the Corso, in the lee of the Campidoglio, substantial changes had to be made to the whole area, which had hitherto ended in the piazza. In 1845 the latter had witnessed the first appearance of a horse omnibus and gas lighting. The next step was the demolition of the buildings sheltered by the monument; this enlarged the piazza, which was extended even further after the demolition

of the 16th century Palazzo Torlonia, opposite Palazzo Venezia. Next the Assicurazioni Generali building was constructed, in the style of the Pauline complex; this was placed further back in the piazza. Palazzo Venezia, which had already been commissioned by Cardinal Pietro Barbo as a prestigious private residence in about 1464, was subjected to considerable changes when Paul II was elected pontiff, to make it fit for a «papal palace». As a residence of the ambassadors of the Venetian Republic in 1564, the palazzo underwent further changes when it passed first of all to the Hapsburg Empire and then, in the Napoleonic period, to the Italic Kingdom, when it became home to the Accademia di Belle Arti directed by Antonio Canova. It was to undergo further changes when, between 1929 and 1943, it was home to the head of government and the Great Council of fascism. Meanwhile the outlook of the piazza had evolved in 1911 with the inauguration of the central Monument and the definitive layout of the area. When the axes of Via del Mare and Via dei Fori Imperiali were opened during the twenty years of fascism, the piazza, which was proclaimed the Forum of Italy, was confirmed in its role as both symbolic and geographical centre of the city.

Left: Giuseppe Sacconi, Monument to Vittorio Emanuele II

Below: Palazzo Venezia

Facing page, below: view of the square from the Monument to Vittorio Emanuele II

THE GESÙ

The Gesù Church is an extremely important example of late 16th century religious architecture and it played a fundamental role in further developments in Rome's sacred architecture in the 17th century. The complex history of the church began in 1537, with the arrival in Rome after an absence of fourteen years of Saint Ignatius of Loyola. He personally chose the place where the mother church of the Order, the Company of Jesus, of which he was the founder, was to be built. It was recognised by Paul III in 1540 and destined to become one of the most powerful of the Counter-Reformation. But many years passed before the scheme for the building was carried out; it needed the economic power of a character like Cardinal Alessandro Farnese, the nephew of Pope Paul III, to drive the building project forward. At the time of its dedication in 1584, the church was the biggest and first completely new one built since the Sack of Rome in 1527. The Gesù Church is also known as the Farnesian Temple. The saying went that Cardinal Farnese possessed the three most beautiful things in Rome: his family palazzo, his daughter Clelia and the Gesù Church. The novelty of the temple conceived by the architect Domenico Vignola is evident above all in the blueprint. The Gesù was the prototype for a kind of temple with a single hall, which was adapted to the liturgical and devotional demands of the Counter-Reformation and Jesuitical preaching in particular.

Two Jesuit architects participated in the design of the volumetric plan of the building, which has a very compressed transept with three side chapels, and is the result of the fusion of the central plan favoured in the Renaissance and the longitudinal one of the ancient Christian tradition. Then, at the end of the 17th century, the temple would be transformed into one of the finest examples of European Baroque, by the wonderful *trompe l'oeil* painting of Giovan Battista Gaulli, or «Baciccio», as he was known.

SANT'ANDREA DELLA VALLE

In 1608 Carlo Maderno, commissioned to revise the project by Pietro Paolo Olivieri, introduced a greater vertical development both internally and externally, of the church considered to be the most important Roman derivative of the church of *Gesù*. The dome, set on an octagonal drum with double columns at the corners, was designed by Maderno in 1622 and is the highest in Rome after Saint Peter's.

Carlo Rainaldi and Carlo Fontana, who designed and built the façade (1656-1665), followed Maderno's project and accentuated its sculptural and decorative aspects; the statues of four saints, (Andrea the Apostle, Andrea of Avellino, Gaetano and Sebastian) stand in the four niches flanking the portal, three of which were sculpted by Domenico Guidi,

while the Andrea of Avellino was sculpted by Ercole Ferrata. Giovanni Lanfranco created an exuberant and complex program for the frescos in the dome, in which the free and dynamic spatial composition of the figures, thanks to the absence of any architectural support, encounters a plastic perception of the bodies that derives from Annibale Carracci and with the special delicacy of the chromatic range. The cycle of frescos kept the artist busy from 1621 to 1627 and was a point of reference for the great illuminist style of decoration. The frescos on the dome pendentives were done by the classicist Domenichino (1623-1628) of Bologna. The tombs of Pius II (early 17th century) and that of Monsignor Giovanni Della Casa (author of *Galateo*) are located inside the church. A follower of Andrea Bregno completed construction of the church between 1470 and 1475.

GALLERIA DORIA PAMPHILJ

The Doria Pamphilj palace houses an extraordinary private gallery of paintings, collected between the 16th and 17th centuries. The kernel of the collection was formed after the marriage of Camillo Pamphilj senior, nephew of pope Innocent X, with Olimpia Aldobrandini in 1647. The bride had, in 1638, inherited the palace on the *Corso* and the art collection from her uncle Ippolito. As early as 1603 the collection already included prestigious paintings by Raphael (*Double portrait of Andrea Navagero and Agostino Beazzano*), and works from the schools of Ferrara and Veneto. Between 1603 and 1604 cardinal Aldobrandini had also had the upper parts of the palace chapel adorned with six arched canvases on which Annibale Carracci and his apprentices had painted landscapes with scenes from the life of Christ, later moved to the gallery.

A better part of the collection is attributable to the Camillo Pamphilj's patronage and collecting activities: in addition to inheriting the properties of his mother Olimpia Maildachini in 1657 including *Ermina Finds the Wounded Tancred* by Guercino, he purchased many works

on the antiques market (including *Flight to Egypt* and *Magdalene* by Caravaggio); he also commissioned important works from artists such as Bernini, Borromini, Pietro da Cortona, Algardi, Duquesnoy, and several Flemish artists. He also purchased landscapes by Lorrain and Dughet, and many paintings from Bologna that now constitute the largest section of the collection The famous *Portrait of Innocent X*, painted by Velázquez during his second trip to Italy (about 1649) was, instead, a gift from the pope to Camillo.

Other paintings were added during the course of the 18th century: these included two portraits of *Andrea Doria* by Sebastiano del Piombo and another of *Giannettino Doria* by Bronzino, and the famous 16th century Brussels tapestries illustrating the *Battle of Lepanto* (1571).

Caravaggio, *Flight to Egypt*

PANTHEON

The Pantheon is stituated in the Roman Regio (quarter) IX, corresponding to Campus Martius. According to legend, Campus Martius used to belong to the Tarquins and was a marshy area.

When the last Etruscan king was expelled from Rome in 509 BC, the year the Republic was founded, the area became public. Augustus began filling the central area of Campus Martius with monuments and rebuilding the buildings in the Circus Flaminius area. The temple – dedicated to all the gods – was intended to be a symbol of the Emperor Augustus and therefore of his family, the gens Iulia.

The Pantheon owes its current appearance to the restructuring conducted by Hadrian between 118 and 125 AD. This maintained the blueprint of the previous construction, except where the level of the base was raised and the width of the pronaos reduced to eight columns. The inscription on the architrave referring to the building of the temple by Agrippa was retained by Hadrian, who never had his name inscribed on any of the monuments he built, with the exception of Trajan's temple.

A second inscription in smaller letters records the restoration by Septimius Severus and Caracalla in 202 AD. In 609 AD the Byzantine Emperor Foca gave the Pantheon to Pope Boniface IV, and the temple was changed into the Chiesa di Santa Maria ad Martyres. A flight of steps led up to a large portico with eight monolithic granite columns with white marble capitals and bases. Two more rows of four columns formed the three aisles.

The monumental bronze door is probably original, although it has been restored many times. The dome is the largest one built prior to the 20th century; it measures 43.30 metres in diameter and was built using a huge wooden framework.

The use of layers of concrete alternated with tufa and pumice served to lessen the weight of the huge structure. The height of the temple from the floor to the top of the dome is equal to the diameter of the latter, meaning that a sphere could fit into the interior, so that there is a perfect balance in the building's proportions. On the inside the dome is adorned with five rows of coffering which were probably originally decorated with gilded bronze elements.

ANDREA POZZO, *GLORY OF SAINT IGNATIUS*

SANT'IGNAZIO

When general Oliva called the thirty-eight year old Andrea Pozzo to Rome in 1680, the Chiesa di Sant'Ignazio, which had been open since 1642, still had a bare and unornamented appearance. Pozzo, who was born in Trento, was a Jesuit and had made his reputation in northern Italy decorating several of the order's churches with impressive effects in terms of perspective. When

he arrived in Rome he devoted himself to the decoration of the church, painting the series of stories of the saint and the Company of Jesus in the corridor of the convent annexe, the pretence dome with projecting architectural motifs (a large flat canvas with painted perspective effects, creating the illusion of an authentic dome, noted at the time as «rather vague and artificial»), the pendentives with their biblical figures, the choir and, lastly, the spectacular nave ceiling. This seems pierced by very sharply foreshortened architectural features which open out in the

centre with the portrayal of the titular saint in glory. The ceiling decoration project began in 1688 and, in this case as well, it was used as a means of celebrating the Jesuits' missionary activity. The light comes from God the Father to the Son, who transmits it to Saint Ignatius, and it splits into four rays leading to the four continents. The figurative and architectural elements merge and the illusionistic details are resolved by the juxtaposition of blinding rays of light and areas of shadow, in a manner reminiscent of Gaulli. The *trompe l'oeil* perspectives of Pozzo, whether in the paintings of the dome, the apse or the Saint Ignatius ceiling, constitute one of the most remarkable legacies of Baroque Rome. With his perspective and the idea of using pretence architecture to expand space, Pozzo also provided an example which was later followed in many Italian, Austrian and German churches of the Jesuit order.

PIAZZA NAVONA

Thanks to its original elongated form, Piazza Navona deserves a foremost place among Rome's numerous historical piazzas. Built on the site of the former Domitian stadium, it traditionally accommodated the market and popular shows. During the 17th century it became the city's salon, partly because of the presence of Palazzo Pamphilj, and it was embellished with further monuments and buildings. These enhance the spatial homogeneity which is owed to the regularity of the architectural features packed into the unbroken ranks of walls and façades, and to the chromatic unity. A result of the urban plans for the piazza under the patronage of Innocent X Pamphilj, who was responsible for the complete reorganisation of the area and the demolition of some blocks, was the concave façade of Sant'Agnese. The work of Borromini, it merges with the walls surrounding the piazza, copying the essential architectural motifs and presenting an emblematic example of dynamic integration between the building and the space in front of it, which acts as an extension to the church and seems to disappear into it. In the layout of the piazza, a role of no lesser importance is played by the three fountains which serve to break up the huge horizontal space into four distinct areas. The focus is the symbolic and actual centre of the Fontana dei Quattro Fiumi (*Fountain of the Four Rivers*), the work of Gian Lorenzo Bernini. It is a spectacular allegory of the worldly prestige of the Pamphilj: an aerial «natural grotto». The four springs of faraway rivers spout from it and it is studded with exotic plants and animals. It acts as a base for the Egyptian obelisk crowned with a dove, the symbol of the Pamphilj and the Holy Spirit.

Facing page: Gian Lorenzo Bernini, Fontana dei Quattro Fiumi

Above: view of the square

Left: Gian Lorenzo Bernini, *Ganges*, detail of the Fontana dei Quattro Fiumi

CARAVAGGIO, *STORIES OF SAINT MATTHEW*

SAN LUIGI DEI FRANCESI

Thanks to the mediation of Cardinal Del Monte from the July of 1599 to that of 1600, Caravaggio painted the two side canvases for the chapel of Cardinal Contarelli in San Luigi dei Francesi, his first public commission. The *Calling* and *Martyrdom of Saint Matthew* were both demanding in terms of the depiction of a story in action and the numerous figures. The symbolic role of the light, coupled with the natural illumination of the chapel, lends unity to the whole. With these canvases Caravaggio brings contemporary reality into a sacred scene and into a church chapel for the first time. Characters dressed in the current style participate in the sacred event as they go about their daily life, intent on tavern games. The first canvas to be finished was the *Calling*. Caravaggio constructs the scene around the gesture of Christ, who points towards Matthew and whose hand position is mirrored by the

latter's. The two groups are unified by the shaft of light, whose origin is outside the field of vision, above the head of Jesus. The light is both divine and natural and also serves as an efficacious stylistic expedient to emphasise the evident contrast between the modern clothes of Matthew and his companions and the few divine attributes of the apostle, who is barefoot and wrapped in a large cloak of antique style. In the case of the *Martyrdom*, the focal point of the scene is the executioner, who is in the act of striking the martyr. The other characters are placed around the central figure, gradually going further back into the bare space which is the scene of the action. Caravaggio freezes the dramatic moment before the death by means of the light. This is concentrated on the naked body of the executioner poised to strike and on the angel who proffers the palm of martyrdom to the saint.

Once it was placed on the altar of the chapel, the altarpiece of Saint Matthew and the Angel, which was done in three and a half months in 1602, was, according to Bellori: «taken away by the priests, who said that the figure had

neither the decorum nor appearance of a saint, with his legs apart and his feet roughly exposed to the people». In fact the image of the saint as an illiterate who seemed to be receiving help with his reading from the angel was too much for the people. So Caravaggio replaced the canvas with a new version which was more in line with the tastes of the priesthood: the saint is no longer a peasant; he emanates wisdom while the angel flies down towards his shoulders.

Facing page: Caravaggio, *Calling of Saint Matthew*, Contarelli chapel

Caravaggio, *Martyrdom of Saint Matthew* and detail, Contarelli chapel

PALAZZO ALTEMPS

The elegant palazzo was built between the end of the 15th and 16th centuries. After the faithful and praiseworthy restoration by the Archeological Service, it now houses some of the antiquities acquired by its former owner, Cardinal Marco Altemps, and numerous works belonging to other fine Roman collections. The sculptures come from the Mattei collection in Villa Celimontana, from the Del Drago collection and from the 17th century Boncompagni-Ludovisi collection. The masterpieces of the latter were restored by prominent baroque artists such as, Gian Lorenzo Bernini and Alessandro Algardi (the *Discus Thrower, Acrolith, Ludovisi Throne, Ares, Juno, Erinyes* and the *Ludovisi sarcophogus*, and the *Galatian and his wife committing suicide*).

Also of great interest are the Egyptian sculptures found in the Santuario di Iside in Campus Martius and the sumptuous Sant'Aniceto church, built in the grounds by Giovanni Angelo Altemps between 1603 and 1618 with frescoes by Pomarancio.

Top of the page: view of the frescoed loggia

Above: *Galatian and his wife committing suicide*

FONTANA DI TREVI

The Fontana di Trevi, a happy and successful marriage of classicism and baroque, was planned as an exhibition of the Acqua Vergine by Nicola Salvi under the patronage of Clement XII. Pope Urban VIII Barberini had already instructed Gian Lorenzo Bernini to «transform» the piazza and the fountain, but the project was never carried out. Set along one side of Palazzo Poli, the fountain, which was made by Nicola Salvi between 1732 and 1763, represents an original and imaginative fusion, in the Berninian style, of architecture, sculpture and the natural elements which contribute to the fountain's unique character. The theme of the sculpture is the sea. The design is dominated by a chariot in the form of a shell in which the great statue of Neptune by Pietro Bracci stands, flanked in the side niches by Health and Plenty, the works of Filippo Della Valle. The chariot is pulled by marine horses, who are in turn preceded by tritons. The marine divinities are placed on rocks of irregular blocks of travertine. The fountain sprawls below the façade of the palazzo behind it, which is in rigidly classicising style, based on the triumphal arch model, with further sculptures in niches as well as in the attic storey and an elegant balustrade. The surrounding houses crowd round the splendid monument, giving the impression of an amphitheatre, while the noise of the fountain's water can be heard from the maze of surrounding streets up to the moment when the snow-white scene appears miraculously before the astonished eyes of the visitor.

VILLA MEDICI
AND PIAZZA DI SPAGNA

The Villa Medici and its big park were created at the end of the 16th century where, in antiquity, there had been the gardens of Lucullus, who was celebrated in Latin literature for his passion for gastronomy and the art of living. Cardinal Ricci acquired the land in 1564, had a palazzo built on it by the Florentine architect Nanni di Baccio Bigio and was responsible for the first significant phase of works. In 1576 Cardinal Ferdinando de' Medici, the great collector and patron, bought the estate and entrusted the Florentine architect Bartolomeo Ammannati with a very ambitious project. Ferdinando de' Medici, a lover of antiquity, conceived the villa as a museum, with a refined gallery-antiquarium. The garden was also planned in a theatrical spirit, on the lines of botanical gardens created by the Medici family in Pisa and Florence. Many rare plants were to be found in it, together with numerous antiquities. The palazzo was only to recover its status as a haven for the arts in the 19th century, when it became the seat of the Académie Française in Rome. Below the villa is the expanse of one of the most picturesque piazzas in Rome, with the theatrical backdrop of the monumental 13th century flight of steps of Trintità dei Monti leading down to the distinctive Barcaccia fountain, which was the work of Pietro Bernini in 1629. The Piazza di Spagna, which forms a splendid background to the Via dei Condotti and is a real «icon» of the city, is one of the most monumental and theatrical urban complexes in Rome. From the 16th century onwards, the space between it and the nearby Via Margutta and Via Babuino was a meeting point for artists and writers, and the area was animated by antique shops, inns and elegant residential buildings. However it was between the seventeenth and eighteenth centuries that the piazza took on its present appearance, with the distinctive «butterfly» shape, formed by two triangles with a common vertex. Having initially been called «alla Trinità», after the church which dominates it, it came to be known as the Piazza di Spagna in reference to the Spanish ambassador's residence there. 1629 was the year in which Pietro Bernini and his son Gian Lorenzo executed the Barcaccia fountain. This was conceived to commemorate the flooding of the Tiber in 1598, and its distinctive boat shape is an allusion to the Church being under the safe guidance of the Barberini. It rests on the ground inside another elliptical-shaped basin, which acts as the spatial pivot of the piazza, but it is the central steps which make this one of the most famous settings of the city. Built by Francesco De Sanctis between 1723 and 1726 under the patronage of Innocent XIII, to resolve the difference in level between the Chiesa di Trinità dei Monti and the piazza below, the Spanish steps are based on the design of the port of Ripetta sul Tevere, which was built in 1704 by Alessandro Specchi and then destroyed. The daring solution is a confirmation of the theatrical bent of late-Baroque urban planning in the capital. It includes impressive balustraded terraces embraced by two wings of steps, which, in an elegant fan motif and alternating and curvilenear movement of converging and diverging ramps, merge to flow down into the piazza below.

View of the internal facade of villa Medici

Facing page: view of the steps and church at Trinità dei Monti

ARA PACIS

To celebrate the victorious return of Augustus from military campaigns in Spain and Gaul, in 13 BC the Senate voted for the construction of a monumental altar for the Augustan Peace, which was dedicated in 9 BC. The monument was built to the west of the Via Flaminia, in the northern part of Campus Martius, an area which was radically remodelled by the Augustan changes. The altar itself was surrounded by a rectangular marble screen, with reliefs sculpted in two sections. On the inside, the upper area is decorated with festoons and sacrificial goblets, while the lower one reproduces in marble the posts of the wooden fence which had originally enclosed the sacred area. On the outside, the slabs of the lower section are covered with extremely elegant acanthus volutes, while in the upper reliefs there are figurative scenes, illustrating fundamental themes of Augustan policy in the style of Greek art of the Classical and Hellenistic age. In the panels on the short sides, where the two entrances are, there are representations of mythological scenes connected to the foundation of Rome and the traditional religion, which Augustus wished to extol. On one side is the grotto known as *Lupercalia*, where the wolf suckled Romulus and Remus, and the sacrifice of Aeneas to the Penates; on the other are personifications of the Earth flourishing thanks to the peace, and of Rome, triumphant under the rule of Augustus. On the long sides is a religious procession, among the participants Augustus, Livia, Agrippa, who had died in 12 BC, and all the members of the imperial family in hierarchical order can be recognised.

The position of each was determined by their relationship to the prince and role in the line of succession. The frieze of the interior altar, which

is crowned with volutes, depicts the canonical sacrifice of the three victims – the pig, the sheep and the bull – which was performed annually in the presence of the Vestal virgins and the most important priests, in a style which is closer to the Roman-Italic tradition.

PIAZZA DEL POPOLO AND SANTA MARIA DEL POPOLO

«You are a world, Rome!» Goethe exclaimed, as soon as he had entered the city by the Porta del Popolo, and, after days of walking, found himself in the harmonious piazza. The huge space, which is closed to the north by the gate of the same name and dominated to the east by the ramp of the Pincio walkway, and is so wisely orchestrated from the point of view of town-planning, architecture, landscaping and urban decoration, evolved in the space of three and a half centuries. Since Medieval times, the church of Santa Maria del Popolo had welcomed the traveller and pilgrim who arrived in the city, weary after days of walking, by the Via Flaminia. It started off as a mere chapel built from the funds of the Roman people; then, in the 13th century Gregory IX enlarged it and in 1250 it underwent further changes when it passed to the Augustinians. However, in the 15th century, from 1472 onwards to be exact, during the pontificate

of Sixtus IV, to mark the occasion of the 1475 Jubilee, the Lombard congregation commissioned its rebuilding in accordance with the canons of contemporary sacred Lombard architecture. Later, significant alterations were made by Bramante, Raphael and Bernini. The decorative and sculptural array with which the church was embellished during the 16th century therefore make it one of the most complete of the Roman churches in terms of examples of the art of the time. The masterpieces left here by some of the most important artists active in Rome from the 16th to the 17th century, from Andrea Sansovino to Bernini, from Caravaggio to Annibale Carracci and Carlo Maratta, create on of the most precious treasure troves of works of art in the city. It was on the occasion of the arrival in Rome of Queen Cristina of Sweden that the area took on its baroque form. Then Alexander VII Chigi renovated the piazza under the wise direction of Gian Lorenzo Bernini, inserting the twin churches of Santa Maria dei Miracoli and Santa Maria

di Montesanto at the mouth of the Corso as a «felicitous and auspicious entrance». After the Baroque splendour, the piazza was altered again by Giuseppe Valadier, according to the criteria of the Enlightenment. Games, fares and popular shows took place in the Piazza del Popolo. It was the starting point for the famous Bàrberi race during the carnival and the site of capital punishment. Under the Napoleonic government a plan was implemented for the addition of buildings on a monumental scale influenced by the revolutionary neoclassisicm of Giuseppe Valadier. The Piazza thus assumed its expanded form, with the two lateral semi-circles and the buildings near the gateway.

Andrea Sansovino,
Monument to cardinal
Ascanio Basso della Rovere

External districts
and the West Bank of the Tiber

1 Caracalla Thermae
2 Santa Sabina
3 Santa Cecilia in Trastevere
4 San Pietro in Montorio
5 Villa Farnesina alla Longara
6 Castel Sant'Angelo

CARACALLA THERMAE

Baths were very common in every part of the Empire in Roman times. Besides the bathing areas and the palaestrae (gyms), they were endowed with gardens, nymphaea, libraries, auditoria, places for shows and games and for keeping food and drinks. These diversions had turned attendance at the baths into the habitual and favourite pastime of the Romans, who spent many hours of the day there, devoting themselves to the care of the body and spirit. The baths became places for social gatherings and centres for the diffusion of culture. During the Imperial Age, the construction of thermal water buildings was an integral part of the political-propaganda programme of the emperors, who required ever bigger and better organised establishments,

a genuine «public service», with free entry for the masses. Caracalla's Baths, which are second only to those of Diocletian, are one of the best preserved thermal complexes of antiquity. Probably planned at the time of Septimus Severus, the baths were inaugurated by Marcus Aurelius Antoninus Basianus, known as Caracalla, in 216 AD, in the 12th *regio* or district (*Piscina Publica*), situated in the southern part of the city. The area had been filled with monuments by the Severi, including a splendid nymphaeum with several storeys, built on the south-western slopes of the Palatine Hill, and the Via Nova, the road leading towards the Baths. They were finished in 235 AD and were still working in 537 AD when, after the siege of Rome by the Goths, the aqueducts were cut off to deprive the city of water.

SANTA SABINA

The Basilica of Santa Sabina is situated on the slopes of the Aventine. Its foundations, which document almost a thousand years of history, testify to the lively building activity, which, in antiquity, had as its backdrop this hill which was then so rich in springs and vegetation. The Roman aristocratic families had built their sumptuous dwellings here, near the two thermal centres. The crypt of Santa Sabina bears the traces of a Christian community, which was given hospitality in the house of a Roman matron, Sabina, who had been converted to Christianity by her slave Serafia and who was subsequently decapitated during the Empire of Vespasiano. Later, in the Early Middle Ages, the Aventine was selected by monks and the religious as the seat of their hermitages or little fraternal communities. In this context, from the

fifth century onwards, one of the most imposing Paleo-Christian basilicas of the city sprang up. The fourth century floor of the former domus is all that remains of it, and it can be viewed through a grating near the entrance to the basilica, but many pieces of walling lie beneath the right aisle. The basilica was built in the fifth century and dedicated to San Domenico in 1222. Some restoration work was carried out in the 15th century, but it was the alterations by Domenico Fontana in 1587, at the time of Sixtus V, and Francesco Borromini in 1643, which would change the interior of the basilical complex fundamentally. Domenico Fontana demolished the *schola cantorum*, the *iconostasis* and the *ciborium*, introducing the main altar and large baldacchino. In the early 20th century Antonio Muñoz eliminated these changes to restore the church to its original appearance. Three spacious aisles with solemn classical proportions, divided up by twenty-four Corinthian columns, create a majestic internal space based on Ravenna prototypes. This is one of the first basilical exemplars where the columns bear arches rather than trabeations. Originally the church was faced in rich mosaics of which only a fragment remains above the door. There is a metrical inscription in gold lettering alluding to Pietro d'Illiria, who built the church, Celestine I, during whose pontificate it was built, and to the Council of Ephesus. The walls of the church were also faced with marble inlay.

SANTA CECILIA IN TRASTEVERE

This basilica was built by Pope Paschal I during the ninth century; the portico, bell tower and cloister in the right wing of the convent were added between the end of the 12th and early 13th centuries; as early as 1540 the church began to be the object of numerous restoration operations up to the most radical one of 1724, executed at the will of cardinal Francesco Acquaviva. The monumental entrance is attributed to Ferdinando Fuga (1741-1742) The portico in front of the façade (somewhat retouched during the 18th century) still has its ancient columns, the original architrave with its mosaic decorations, tombstones and medieval fragments.

Inside there are three naves: the central nave, with its lowered barrel vault terminating in an apse, is separated from the side aisles by pilasters that incorporate the ancient columns. The tabernacle by Arnolfo di Cambio (1293) at the center of the presbytery is a true masterpiece of Gothic architecture and sculpture. Among the marble statues, *Saint Cecilia* by Stefano Maderno (1600), portrayed in the act of recognition, is particularly worthy of admiration.

The *Universal Judgement* frescos by Pietro Cavallini in the Nuns' Choir, built on the internal face of the façade, are considered to be his masterpiece and the most significant work of Roman painting prior to Giotto.

Arnolfo di Cambio,
Tabernacle

PIETRO CAVALLINI, *UNIVERSAL JUDGEMENT*

SANTA CECILIA IN TRASTEVERE

It was the rediscovery, in 1899, of the surviving frescoes by Cavallini in the convent of Santa Cecilia, which brought up the problem of the identity of the Roman painter. He was celebrated by Ghiberti in his *Commentari* as the most important of his time, and mention was made of a substantial group of works attributed to him and now mainly lost. The most representative work of Pietro Cavallini is in fact the cycle of frescoes in Santa Cecilia in Trastevere, which were probably executed in the same period as the Arnolfian ciborium, in about 1293. In the *Judgement*, Cavallini distances himself from, and surpasses, the Byzantine vision. Either side of the mandorla containing Christ, the figures of the apostles are placed on thrones, which are painted in perspective. The rhythm of the composition is influenced by a dimension of restrained classicism which has none of the crowding and narrative detail of Byzantine painting. Monumentality and solemnity are new elements in Cavallinian painting. The faces of Christ and the apostles seem modelled by a delicate rapport of light and shadow. Compared to the mosaic in Santa Maria in Trastevere, the fresco technique also gave the painter more stylistic freedom in the representation of drapery, which is soft and

natural, with greater chiaroscuro.

The work therefore acquires a three-dimensional quality and an expressive power of greater dramatic depth. The expressionistic interpretation of the figures is replaced with a typically Western rationalisation of humanity.

Facing page: Pietro Cavallini, Seraphim, and below: Face of Christ, details of the Universal Judgement

SAN PIETRO IN MONTORIO: BRAMANTE'S TEMPIETTO

Built on the top of the Gianicolo, the *tempietto* (little temple) was commissioned by the King of Spain to consecrate the place in which, according to medieval tradition, Saint Peter, the martyr, founder of the Christian Church and first pope, had been crucified. The young architect Bramante conceived it as a genuine *martyrium* in antique style, with a central plan and a circle of perimeter columns. The building must have been placed in a large square, which, however, was never built. In spite of the reduced size, the space has been planned in grandiose, monumental style. It is evidently based on the study of the rules of harmony of the Roman Vitruvius, who advised the use of the Doric order of columns for buildings dedicated to masculine divinities or mythological figures famous for their strength and courage. The architect Bramante did in fact use the Doric order for the tempietto, giving it an air of rigour and economy, which is also due to limited use of excessive decoration and the sober harmony of the volumes.

Facing page:
Sebastiano del Piombo,
Flagellation,
San Pietro in Montorio

VILLA FARNESINA ALLA LONGARA

The Villa Farnesina, one of the jewels of early 16th century Roman classicism, was known as the «Incomparable matchless pearl». It was built in the Trastevere rione between 1506 and 1510, with alterations which lasted until 1520, by Baldassarre Peruzzi, for the Sienese banker, Agostino Chigi. In 1590 it passed to the Farnese, from whom it took its present name. It was the first noble suburban villa in Rome and is a model of balance, harmony and proportion. It has two floors and is in the shape of a horseshoe, which opens onto the garden with a ground floor loggia made up of five arches, which now have protective glass.

Below, left: Raphael, Venus, Ceres and Juno; right: Cupid and the Graces

Facing page: Raphael, Triumph of Galatea

The loggia was used as a stage for festivities and theatrical performances organised by the owner, which contemporaries recall as being particularly sumptuous. The façade has two tiers, superimposed by Doric pilasters strips, and is crowned by a tall frieze sculpted with festoons of cherubs. Baldassarre Peruzzi was also very much involved with the interior painted and stucco-work decoration. These reveal the same skill in perspective as the wall frescoes, which depict external spaces, making external nature and the interior spaces of the villa seem one. The loggia, in particular, painted with a braid of festoons, was treated as a continuum of the garden. It is decorated with frescoes of the story of *Cupid and Psyche*, from Apuleius, by Raphael and his pupils. Besides Raphael, Sebastiano del Piombo also worked on the Sala di Galatea, adjoining the loggia, with its Peruzzi ceiling. This is articulated in geometric spaces divided by painted architectural elements which link to the walls. On the floor above is the Salone delle Prospettive (room of views) painted with a *trompe l'oeil* loggia; between the pretence architectural features there are Roman *trompe l'oeil* landscapes including a vista of Trastevere. Now the villa houses the Accademia dei Lincei and the Gabinetto dei Disegni e delle Stampe, the national graphic collection.

CASTEL SANT'ANGELO

The Tiber is dominated by the impressive Mole of Hadrian, built at the behest of the Emperor, probably designed by him and conceived as his personal mausoleum and tomb. Begun in about 123 AD and finished a year after the death of the Emperor by Antoninus Pius, it became the burial place of the Roman emperors up to Caracalla. To reach the mausoleum Hadrian had a bridge specially built opposite the entrance to the majestic building. The mausoleum was in the form of a square at whose corners there were statuary groups. Today the corners of the massive structure are reinforced by bastions erected in the course of the 16th century on the Pope's wishes, and there are monuments which increase the security and isolation of the mausoleum, which had the appearance of a small fortified village. The tour of the museum inside includes superb cycles of frescoes from the School of Raphael, such as the frieze by Perin del Vaga recounting the tale of *Cupid and Psyche*, from 1545-1547, and the frescoes of the apartment of Pope Paul III which are attributed to the young Pellegrino Tibaldi.

Vatican City

SAINT PETER'S SQUARE

Emerging from the maze of streets and narrow, unhealthy alleys of the Borgo rione, the visitor of the past left behind them the so-called *spina* (thorn), which, as can be seen in photographs of the time, closed the opening of Saint Peter's Square up to the 1930s. Suddenly, in all its splendour, the vast square of Saint Peter appeared in front of them. As part of a project proposed in about 1932 by Marcello Piacentini, but only finished in the Holy Year of 1950, the long stretch of Via della Conciliazione was opened.

Although the new solution privileged view from a distance of the façade and dome, on the other hand it diminished the effect of unexpectedness, the grand reception which had enchanted visitors for centuries. This was the final act in the definitive transformation of the area of Saint Peter's Square which had developed gradually in the course of the centuries. In 1586, Sixtus V was the first to endow the space with a theatrical and monumental aspect, when he engaged Domenico Fontana to move the red granite obelisque to the centre of the piazza, whose symbolic focal point it then became.

Gian Lorenzo Bernini, commissioned by Alessandro VII Chigi, studied the new layout of the piazza, on which he worked for ten years from 1657 to 1667, turning it into one of the most spectacular architectural achievements of Baroque Rome. Starting with a choice which revealed his classical vocation, Bernini replaced the Corinthian order with Doric columns, placing them in such a way as to form three passages, the middle one having wider barrel vaulting and the side ones narrower, coffered ceilings. There are two hundred and eighty-four columns and eighty travertine piers in all, and a trabeation crowned by a series of one hundred and forty statues of saints and six large coats of arms of Pope Chigi.

To avoid a possible effect of disequilibrium due to the use of the crescent and, at the same time, to orchestrate the piazza from the point of view of perspective, Bernini placed the four rows of columns radially, and gradually increased their diameter, thus ensuring that the proportional relations between the spaces and the columns also remained unchanged in the outside row.

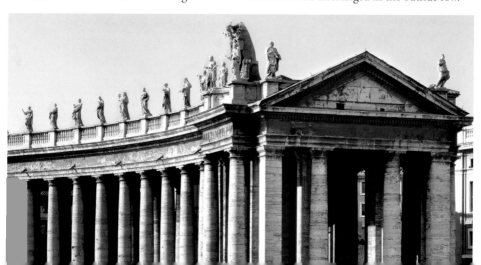

SAINT PETER'S

It was the Emperor Constantine who instigated the construction of the first basilica, in about the year 320, on the site traditionally thought to be that of the tomb of the apostle Peter. It was finished at the time of the pontiff Liberius (352-366) and its layout has been handed down through iconographic and documentary sources. A building with a basilica's blueprint, it was articulated in five aisles and ended in a transept defined on both sides by exedras. Access was gained through a vast quadriportico atrium, the façade of which gave on to the loggia of the Blessings. On the side of the entrance of the quadriportico was the famous *Navicella* mosaic by Giotto and his school. Embellished by furnishings, mosaics and monuments in the course of the Middle Ages, it was in the 15th century that the antique basilica attained its greatest splendour, housing important funerary monuments made by the major artists of the time. On the other hand, serious subsidence problems were threatening the fabric of the building at the time when Pope Nicholas decided to rebuild and enlarge the church, but his death in 1455 led to the works being suspended. In the early 16th century Julius II engaged Donato Bramante to plan the reconstruction of the building, which,

apart from housing his own mausoleum, was intended to signal the definitive triumph of a Rome restored to splendour as the ancient imperial city, and capital of Christianity and of the Church State. Bramante conceived the new Saint Peter's as a monumental organism in the form of a Greek cross contained within a square, crowned with a central semi-spherical dome. In form and diameter it was to be similar to that of the Pantheon, and surrounded by four smaller domes inserted between four minor arms, completed by four corner bell towers. After Bramante died suddenly in 1514, Leo X engaged Raphael to continue with the construction, then Antonio da Sangallo and

finally, in 1546, Michelangelo. The latter went back to the design of Bramante and conceived of a building in the grand style, but simplified in form, covered by a dome which was intended as the central element of the complex. Modelled almost in the same way as a sculpture, the Michelangelesque dome is vibrant, elastic and imposing. Giacomo Della Porta finished it in 1598, keeping to the general lines of the model left by Michelangelo, without following them with complete fidelity, but rather emphasising the verticalism. With Pope Paul V, the basilica took on its final appearance, until on 18th November 1626, Urban VIII celebrated the consecration of the new temple.

MICHELANGELO, *PIETÀ*
SAINT PETER'S

In 1498 Cardinal Bilhéres de Lagraulas, Abbot of San Dionigi and Ambassador of Charles VIII, gave Buonarroti the commission for the very famous sculptural group, which was to be placed in the chapel of Santa Petronilla in the ancient Basilica of Saint Peter. The same patron asked the artist to follow a northern iconographic model of the Virgin holding the body of her son in her arms after the deposition from the cross. As opposed to the composition of the German original, frozen in an unnatural scheme, Michelangelo, however, preferred to create an image of extreme naturalness, with soft, fluid lines. It is the only work signed by him, on the sash which crosses the Virgin's breast. The signature, according to Vasari, indicated the pride of the artist in his achievement. The lyrical intensity of the work, the refined smoothness of the marble and the plasticity of the forms all contribute to make it a work of perfect equilibrium. The absorbed expression on the face of Mary reveals her withheld grief; the body of Jesus, surrendered in exhaustion to the immense pain it has borne, brings the holy scene into the dimension of humanity; the fineness of the garments, the monumental composition and the perfection of the features and anatomy endow the scene with a divine aura and timelessness. Perhaps it was this «absolute» beauty which led to the famous episode so frequently mentioned since, when, on Whit Sunday, May 21 1972, a madman attacked the group with a hammer, entailing a lengthy period of restoration to repair the damage and fill the holes.

GIAN LORENZO BERNINI, *BALDACCHINO*
SAINT PETER'S

As soon as he was elected pontiff, Urban VIII, of the powerful Barberini family, chose Gian Lorenzo Bernini, the sculptor and painter, to take charge of the works required to finish Saint Peter's. In particular, he was to be responsible for the «larger structure» which was to tower above the centre of the presbytery, the high altar, under the Michelangelesque dome. The vast size of the architectural feature cum sculpture which Bernini produced is not immediately noticeable, both because of the well-balanced proportions and because of the rich decoration with which the surfaces of the splendid baldacchino are encrusted. It confirmed the artist as the interpreter who had a greater capacity than any other to translate

the figurative baroque image of the Church triumphant into form. With imagination, ingeniousness and clever planning, he invented the artifice with unequalled virtuosity, enlisting nature, light and space in his theatrical production. He was constantly searching for dramatic effects, trying to combine all the arts in a single work, in which the light was very skilfully controlled. When it was finished in 1633, the baldacchino, which glorified God the Father as well as the Barberini line, had already made a great impression on his contemporaries thanks to its merits: the richness of the contrasts – the play of bronze-coloured black and gold; the unequalled size – it was over 28 metres high; the dynamism of the forms, which simulate the movement of the canopy; the inextricable fusion of sculpture and architecture in this brilliant transcendence of the borders between the arts.

THE APSE CATHEDRA
SAINT PETER'S

Although it is equal in size to the arms of the transept, the apse seems larger and more majestic, as it is joined on to the nave and seems like an extension of it.

Between the two great background pilaster strips, the Chair of Peter towers over the apse. Between 1656 and 1665, this triumphant vision of bronze and gilt, fruit of the baroque genius of Gian Lorenzo Bernini, was executed under the patronage of Alexander VII Chigi. Within the bronze structure is the ancient wooden chair claimed by legend to be that of Saint Peter.

The architecture is vibrant and rather than appearing superimposed on the structure of the building, the artist's design is like a festive decoration.

Held up by four imposing figures of saints, the chair seems chiselled and is decorated with golden arabesques.

Above it, Bernini exploits the source of light from the central window of the apse, creating a glorious swirling group of angels and cherubs, amongst clouds and dazzling rays, flying round the window featuring the dove of the Holy Spirit. Bernini's work embodies the idea, with all its nuances, of the felicitous union of painting, sculpture and architecture in a single work, in the manner of the poetics of synthesis of Filippo Baldinucci.

The imposing papal tombs of Paul III Farnese and Urban VIII Barberini are on either side of the apse in large niches.

VATICAN MUSEUMS

Often identified simply as being limited to Raphael's Rooms and Michelangelo's frescos in the Sistine Chapel, the Vatican Museums actually offer kilometers of historical, artistic and cultural itineraries of great breadth and interest: from Egyptian and Etruscan art to contemporary graphics, passing through antique statues, Italian painting from the last seven centuries, and even papal carriages. The history of the Vatican Museums is intimately linked to two factors: the will of the enthroned popes over the past five hundred years and the architectural variations of Vatican palaces. Important expansions and renovations of the complex go back to the middle of the 15th century, when the Vatican became the official papal residence, and continued during the same century with the foundation of the Vatican Library and the construction of the Sistine Chapel. The first space built expressly to exhibit works of art was built at the behest of Julius II: in 1503 the pope commissioned Donato Bramante to execute important works, including the construction of the magnificent Belvedere court and the adjacent Court of the Statues where the masterpieces of ancient statues were exhibited. During the 18th and 19th centuries major additions were made to the collections; the need to protect the priceless artistic estate induced the popes to prepare

new exhibition spaces for ancient statues, such as the Pio-Clementine and Chiaramonti museums (Museo Pio-Clementino and Museo Chiaramonti) which housed works such as *Laocoon* and *Apollo del Belvedere*, previously in the Belvedere court. Thanks to the edict issued by cardinal Pacca in 1820, which regulated the archeological excavations and entitled public collections to a sort of right of pre-emption for their finds, in 1837 it was possible to inaugurate the Gregorian Etruscan museum (Museo Gregoriano Etrusco) with valuable materials unearthed during the extensive excavations conducted during the early 19th century in southern Etruria, under the jurisdiction of the Papal States at that time. In 1839 the Gregorian Egyptian Museum (Museo Gregoriano Egizio) was also opened. After 1870, when these territories were excluded from the Papal States and, consequently, the protective constraints were no longer applicable, the Vatican Museums were principally occupied with renewing the layout of the estate accumulated through the centuries. The opening of the Gallery inaugurated in 1932 and still existing today, dates back to this phase. Attention to missionary work and the modern evangelistic function of the Church also led to the foundation of special collections, such as the Missionary-Ethnology Museum (Museo Missionario-Etnologico) and the Collection of Contemporary Art (Collezione d'Arte Contemporanea).

LAOCOON
PIO-CLEMENTINE MUSEUM

The famous sculptural group was found in a vineyard on the Esquiline Hill on 14th January 1506. The work lauded by Pliny the Elder as part of the sculptural furnishing of the Palazzo di Tito was made by the Rhodes sculptors Athanadoros, Hagesandros and Polydoros. The marble was acquired by Pope Julius II in the year of its discovery and placed in the Belvedere Vatican courtyard. The right arm of the central figure, which had been lost at the time of the discovery of the group, which was incorrectly reassembled in the 17th century, was recovered by the archaeologist Ludwig Pollak from a Roman stone cutter's workshop in 1905. The work shows Laocoon with his two sons being killed by sea serpents near a shrine, for having cast doubt on the divine nature of the gift of the Trojan horse. The figures are portrayed as already immobilised by the coils of the serpents who have killed the younger son and wounded the father in the left side; the elder son tries in a vain to free himself from the mortal grasp. The discovery of the monumental sculptural groups in the Grotta di Sperlonga, part of the Villa of Tiberius, signed by the same authors as the Laocoon, has fuelled the debate about the work's origin as a Hellenistic original or a copy made at the time of Tiberius from a bronze model of the second half of the second century BC.

VATICAN PINACOTECA

Within the articulated complex of the Vatican Museums, the Gallery founded by Pius VI includes a valuable nucleus of paintings, for the most part with sacred subjects, from the Middle Ages up to the 18th century. Most of these works were taken away by the French after the signing of the Tolentino treaty in 1797 and were only partly recovered in 1816 by Antonio Canova.

The definitive museum of the collection is located in the palace built by Pius XI according to Luca Beltrami's project of 1932. New acquisitions to the original nucleus have been added over time. The itinerary of the exhibition winds through eighteen halls and the works are displayed in chronological order. The first two rooms are dedicated to medieval painting, from the Italian primitives to Giotto and his followers, up to late Gothic. Five rooms are dedicated to the 15th century: works range from such masters as Beato Angelico, Filippo Lippi, Benozzo Gozzoli, to Palmezzano and Melozzo di Forlì (including the famous fragments of frescos from the basilica of the Holy Apostles and from the ancient Vatican Library), up to the artists who represent the Emilia region during the 15th century (Ercole de' Roberti, Carlo Crivelli) and those from the Umbria school (Perugino). The eighth hall, the largest in the gallery, is entirely dedicated to the works of Raphael: in fact the ten tapestries made in Brussels, to cartoons of the artist from Urbino, for the Sistine Chapel, and some of his most famous paintings (*Transfiguration, Madonna di Foligno, Incoronation of the Virgin*) hang here. Leonardo and other 16th century artists occupy the next room, while the tenth room houses 16th century Venetian painting and paintings by Titian. In addition to paintings of the late 16th century, the itinerary continues with some important masterpieces of the 17th and 18th centuries.

RAPHAEL, *MADONNA DI FOLIGNO*
VATICAN PINACOTECA

The great fame Raphael acquired so quickly in Rome, as a result of his commission to decorate the rooms in the Vatican Palaces, led to his being sought out by many important personages in the ecclesiastical hierarchy, as well as those connected to the papal court and the intellectual ambience, who entrusted him with prestigious commissions. One of them was this painting, which Raphael produced between the end of 1511 and the following year, under the patronage of the historian, Sigismondo de' Conti, who was secretary to Julius II and head of the works in Saint Peter's. The work had formerly been on the main altar of the Roman Church of Santa Maria in Aracoeli, where the patron was buried in February 1512, and it was moved by a niece of Sigismondo to the monastery of Sant'Anna di Foligno where she was a nun (hence the derivation of the name by which the painting is commonly known). The panel was taken to Paris in 1797 and, after being given back to the monastery in Foligno, became part of the Vatican collection. The painting features the Virgin and Child seated on a cloud, together with saints who occupy the foreground and the patron kneeling. Instead of the traditional scheme for the sacred conversations, in which the Madonna is usually presented seated on a throne, Raphael uses a different compositional effect, with the divinity high in the sky. Raphael infuses the whole composition with an intense devotional elation, through the cumulative effect of the individual characters' gestures. His aim was to involve the faithful more directly.

RAPHAEL'S ROOMS

Raphael's great opportunity came in 1508. At the time, Giuliano della Rovere, Pope Julius II, decided to move to the upper floor of the Vatican Palaces, where there were four new rooms to renovate in the northern area. The work was entrusted to Bramante and began in the Stanza della Segnatura (Room of the Signature) and the Pontiff engaged some of the most well-known artists of the time, among whom was the young Raphael. The artist's success was immediate: the Pope decreed that «all the other masters both old and young should be thrown to the winds» and entrusted the entire decoration to the young man from Urbino. In the Stanza della Segnatura, the space dedicated to the pontiff's library, Raphael departed from the most well known iconographic precedents for his scheme, painting a sequence of ideal portraits of figures as symbols of knowledge and making them part of a choral action. This was a visual manifestation of the organising concept which informed the union between antique knowledge and Christian revelation. The arrangement of the crowds, the final balance of forces and the space assigned to every detail convey the idea of a spiritual order, which is inherent in all the frescoes in the Stanze. A great airiness, the harmonious juxtaposition of subtle chromatic ranges and accurately studied gestures are salient features of the compositions. In the complex iconographic programme of the rooms,

both the spiritual and temporal power of the Church had to be affirmed, with emphasis on the ideal continuity between the greatness of antique Rome and modern, Christian Rome. In all the frescoes of the first two rooms, the artist demonstrates his capacity to respond to the pontiff's demands with new iconographic solutions, but Julius II died in Rome in February 1513. Raphael then received the commission for the third room, which takes its name from the episode depicted in the only fresco by him for it: the *Fire in the Borgo* (circa 1514). Critics of the artist have noted the beginning of a new pictorial style in this work, characterised by a heroic sense of classicism and by new preoccupations, which signals the arrival of Mannerism.

Above and facing page:
Raphael, *Liberation of Saint Peter* and detail

Following pages: Raphael, *Fire in the Borgo*

RAPHAEL, *SCHOOL OF ATHENS*
RAPHAEL'S ROOMS

In the *School of Athens* (1509), Raphael affirms the centrality of the rational search for the truth, besides receptiveness towards the wisdom of the ancients, which is celebrated here, in the context of the decorative project for the rooms of a Catholic Pope in the Renaissance Age. The philosophers and sages of antiquity are placed within the splendid classical architecture. In the centre are the figures of Plato and Aristotle, indicating the sky and the earth respectively. The measured and eloquent gestures signify philosophy, and the faces of Raphael's contemporaries are used for the sages of the past: Michelangelo, who was painting the ceiling of the Sistine Chapel at the same time, is recognisable in the figure of Heraclitus, seated and leaning with his left elbow on the first step of the staircase. The perspective creates a very effective framework for the scene, enabling an immediate reading of the message and role of the characters represented. This is aided by the light which floods the scene, infusing it with solemnity and clarity. In short, this scenario in the grand style celebrates the continuity between the antique and the modern, the great philosophy of the pagan age and the greatness of the Church.

FIFTEENTH-CENTURY FRESCOES
SISTINE CHAPEL

The explicit purpose of the iconographic programme of the Sistine Chapel, which was built in the Vatican Palaces complex between 1477 and 1481, to the design of the architect Baccio Pontelli, was to underline the pontifical authority of Sixtus IV della Rovere who was invested in 1471. The team of Florentine artists engaged by the Pope for the enterprise is thought by modern critics to have been led by Perugino, who only began to work in 1480 on establishing the general criteria for the work, the architectural divisions and the dimensions of the figures. From the summer of 1481, Cosimo Rosselli, Botticelli and Ghirlandaio were also engaged. Luca Signorelli and Bartolomeo della Gatta were taken on at the end, and executed, respectively, the *Last Days of Moses* and the lost *Dispute between Saint Michael and the Devil*, works of an extraordinary plastic and inventive power and which exercised no little influence over Michelangelo for the ceiling. Perugino was entrusted with the most important fresco from the doctrinal point of view, the *Donation of the Keys*, and it is not by chance that his portrait appears beside that of the two architects. The only signature to appear in the whole cycle is also that of the Umbrian master, in the *Baptism of Christ*. In the middle section on the right are the *Stories of Christ* and on the left, those of Moses, so that they are opposite one another. The inscriptions above each scene have an explanatory function and are intended to underline the way in which the Moses story prefigures that of Christ. The focal point of the whole cycle is in fact the *Donation of the Keys*,

which reveals how Perugino has assimilated the geometric-mathematical concept of Piero della Francesca. The episode is constructed around a central axis whose visual counterpoint is the top of the tympanum of the Temple of Solomon, depicted in the background, while the shiny expanse of the marble inlay in the square is designed with the geometric device of vanishing points. The scene is very evocative and is arranged by Perugino in perfect symmetry: the two triumphal arches stand out on the line of the horizon; in the piazza, two groups of little figures seem to portray some other episodes from the Gospels, while in the foreground there are two groups of onlookers who act as wings to the central scene. Set beside the measured compositional order of Perugino is the restless imagination of Botticelli, author of the scene of the *Punishment of Korah, Dathan and Abiram*. The allusion to those who rebel against Moses is intended to drive home the legitimacy of the supremacy of the Roman Church and the papacy.

Above: Sandro Botticelli, *Punishment of Korah, Dathan and Abiram*

Below: Perugino, *Donation of the Keys*

MICHELANGELO, THE FRESCOED CEILING
SISTINE CHAPEL

In 1504, the chapel begun by Sixtus IV in 1477 had revealed serious movement problems, which necessitated consolidation works. Iron chains were inserted into the ceiling with its painted, starry sky and the filling of holes resulted in damage to the former decoration. For this reason Julius II decided to have new frescoes executed by Michelangelo. The iconographic programme was to include the depiction of stories from Genesis, the Prophets and the Ancestors of Christ, and other allegorical figures. In this way the ceiling became the ideal preface to the 15th century narrative cycle on the walls, with the stories of Moses, Jesus and the pontiffs. The work began in 1508 and was carried out almost exclusively by Michelangelo until 1512. The monumental figures are depicted within an architectural cornice in the grand style. This unifies the separate parts, conceived as a succession of triumphal arches, which mark out the route of the pontifical procession from the entrance to the altar. The narrative begins with the vigorous figures of the Prophets and the Sibyls, portrayed on the side walls in larger dimensions than the others, muscular and powerful, in various attitudes, some in absorbed meditation and others caught up in vibrant dynamism. In the central section of the ceiling, Michelangelo depicts nine stories taken from the Book of Genesis. The artist wanted the scenes to be read in reverse order, from those of the creation to the stories of Noah, from whom the Jewish race is descended. However the focal point of the narrative is the *Creation of Adam*; it is known worldwide and is an emblem of the perfect classicism which informs Renaissance culture. The whole composition is constructed on transversal lines which run parallel or intercept each other, making the two bodies seem drawn to one another. The tale of Genesis then continues, with the depiction of the stock originating from the three sons of Noah; these are the Ancestors of Christ depicted in the vaulting cells and the lunettes. In the latter in particular, Michelangelo experiments with some of the more innovative solutions of the Sistine cycle. The characters portrayed have a great variety of temperaments; some seemed to ignore the observer, absorbed in private contemplation. The colours are more varied, while the artist's technique is freer and more spontaneous.

MICHELANGELO, *UNIVERSAL JUDGEMENT*
SISTINE CHAPEL

In 1533, Clement VII was the first person to suggest to Michelangelo that he should paint the *Judgement* on the walls of the Sistine Chapel. When the Medici pontiff died, the plan was taken up by his successor, Paul III Farnese. The artist began to put up the scaffolding in June 1535. He covered the walls with a layer of bricks, which were thicker at the top than the bottom, so as to produce an inclined surface which would make the work easier to read and avoid dust deposits. A single large compositional structure contains the *Judgement*, although there is no architectural framework whatsoever: the various parts, from top to bottom, are connected and refer to each other. The sky, painted with lapislazuli, a material as incorruptible and precious as gold, brings unity to the different parts of the scene and has a symbolic function, transporting the vision outside time. Angels with the symbols of

the passion are depicted in the top of the lunettes. In the centre, Christ in Judgement and Mary are surrounded by the ranks of the blessed and the saints. In the middle section, angels sound the trumpets of Judgement, while at the sides the just rise upwards and the damned are driven down to the infernal Gods. The last scenes, in the lowest section, portray the resurrection of the bodies and the damned being led to Hell. In 1564, after the Council of Trent, Daniele da Volterra was engaged to add the famous «breeches», to cover what appeared at the time as the excessive nudity of the *Judgement*. In the recent restoration (1990-1994) some of Volterra's alterations – those applied dry – were eliminated, and, after lengthy cleaning, the fresco has recovered its luminosity and clarity of colours and forms in such a way as to regain both definition in the details and an overall unity of the work. This extraordinary Dantesque vision, this manifestation of the horror of merciless divine judgement, is a clear reference to the church's need to reflect on the destructive events of the Sack of Rome (1527), but it speaks a universal language which propels it well beyond its time, making it capable of reflecting the melancholy and fear, anguish and hope, eroticism and pain, individual and collective tragedy, of contemporary humanity.

BEATO ANGELICO, FRESCOES
CAPPELLA NICCOLINA

In 1447, a few months after gaining the papal seat, Nicholas V called the Florentine painter to Rome, to decorate a small area of the Vatican Palaces for use as a private chapel for the pontiff. This is how, together with the aid of collaborators, Beato Angelico came to paint the frescoes of the *Stories of Saint Stephen and Saint Lawrence*, heroes of early Christianity and witnesses of the transition from the still pagan world to the beginning of Christianity. The setting for the scenes is an ideal city, with Renaissance buildings beside those of antiquity. The figures wear modern clothes and there are allusions to living personages; for example, Pope Sixtus II has the face of Nicholas V himself. A noble, almost monumental tone pervades the frescoes of Angelico, from the sculptural definition of the characters to the almost grandiose and cultured architecture with its, in some cases, daring foreshortening. The perfect architectural framework and the solidity of the bodies are the perfect expression of the concept of Christian Humanism, which the pontiff himself advocated. The aim was to reconcile the antique and Christian cultures and to legitimise papal Rome as the heir of Imperial Rome. Beato Angelico's interest in architecture and perspective is also revealed in the scene where *Saint Lawrence receives the Treasures of the Church from pope Sixtus II*, in which a colonnade hides the Pope from the two armed men entering by a classical doorway, which bears a relief of the Eternal Father on the tympanum. The tale unfolds with an oratorical, and, in some

cases, almost fairy-tale-like tone, while the setting appears to reflect the principles of richness, variety and colour, which, in the words of Alberti, give a building «a light and pleasing air». The moderation and order of Florentine Renaissance art are blended with the humanistic culture rich in archeological and architectural passions promoted by Nicholas V himself.

Above: Beato Angelico, *Saint Lawrence distributing alms*

Below: Beato Angelico, *Saint Lawrence ordained deacon* and *Saint Lawrence receives the Treasures of the Church from pope Sixtus II*

Outside the Walls
from North to South

1 Villa Borghese
2 Museo Nazionale Etrusco
  di Villa Giulia
3 Galleria Nazionale di Arte Moderna

4 Catacomb of San Sebastiano
5 Catacomb of Saint Callixtus
6 Catacombs of Domitilla
7 San Paolo fuori le Mura

GALLERIA AND MUSEUMS OF VILLA BORGHESE

Among the various museums located in the Villa Borghese complex, the most important is undoubtedly Galleria Borghese, situated in the *Casino nobile* (lodge) of the 17th century villa built for cardinal Scipione, where the important collection of painting and sculpture gathered during the 17th century, later integrated by acquisitions of the 18th and 19th centuries, is exhibited.

Today the itinerary through the gallery includes eight rooms on the ground floor as well as the great entrance hall and the chapel, with statues in the center of the rooms, surrounded by the paintings on the walls and the decorations of the ceilings, which constituted the thematic thread of the 18th century layout as well. In the entrance hall late Roman statues line the walls, while the Roman statue of *Marco Curzio*, restored by Pietro Bernini, occupies the back wall. Canova's *Pauline Bonaparte as Venus Victrix* may be admired in the hall known as *del Vaso* (of the vase).

The room of the Sun (*del Sole*) houses painting and sculpture such as Bernini's *David*, a painting by Battistello, and two controversial Still-lifes, attributed to Caravaggio by Zeri. Six of the twelve paintings by Caravaggio owned by Scipione hand in the room of Silenus (*del Sileno*).

The upper storey of the gallery, with thirteen additional rooms, focuses principally on paintings, exhibited in chronological order and by schools. Thus it is possible to retrace the principal phases of Italian and Flemish painting between the fifteenth and 18th centuries, including many absolute masterpieces (Antonello da Messina, Raphael, Titian, Correggio, Guido Reni, Gian Lorenzo Bernini, Rubens, Pietro da Cortona).

In addition to Galleria Borghese, the villa also houses the refined *Casa Museo* (home museum) of the sculptor Pietro Canonica, in the 17th century construction by Gallinaro, known as the *Fortezzuola* (little fort) after it was transformed to a medieval style by the Asprucci's in 1793.

The *Museo Carlo Bilotti*, opened quite recently, is housed in the ex-Orangerie of the villa known as *Casino dei Giochi d'Acqua* (fountains) during the 18th century.

These rooms house the collection donated by the museum's namesake, an Italo-American entrepreneur and internationally known collector, including a numerous nucleus of paintings and sculptures by Giorgio de Chirico, Andy Warhol, Gino Severini and Giacomo Manzù.

TITIAN, *SACRED AND PROFANE LOVE*
GALLERIA BORGHESE

The work was painted by Titian in 1514, when he was 25 years old, for the wedding between Nicolò Aurelio, the Venetian Secretary of the Council of Ten, whose coat of arms is represented on the sarcophagus and Laura Bagarotto, daughter of the judge, from Padova. A fountain decorated with bas relief like an antique sarcophagus fills the long side of the canvas, dividing the painting into two parts. Another caesura is caused by the branches behind the cherub who is stirring the water with his arm. The background is also unusual; on one side there is a church and a flock of sheep, and on the other a fortified city and two rabbits, symbols of love and fertility. Critics have long discussed the marked contrast between the two female figures seated on the edge of the fountain, a contrast which had an illustrious precedent.

In fact Pliny recounts that the Greek sculptor Praxiteles had made two sublime statues of Venus, one clothed and one without clothes. The two equally perfect women symbolise on the one hand «brief earthly happiness», with the attribute of the pot of jewels, and the other «eternal heavenly happiness», holding the burning flame of God's love in her hand. The dressed Venus should therefore probably be interpreted as the pure bride who, close to Love, is assisted by the goddess Aphrodite in person. The gesture of the cherub stirring the water, source of life, in a sarcophagus, therefore probably represents love as intermediary between heaven and earth.
The title is the result of a late 18th century interpretation based on a moralistic reading of the clothed figure. The universal fame of Titian's work was confirmed in 1899, when Rothschilds the bankers offered a greater price for this painting than the estimated worth of the whole of Villa Borghese including the works of art.

CARAVAGGIO, *DAVID WITH THE HEAD OF GOLIATH*
GALLERIA BORGHESE

A three-quarters view of David is presented, emerging from behind a dark curtain, sword in hand and proudly intent on observing the head of Goliath, still bleeding after the decapitation. Although the head of the giant is already severed, it is still strongly expressive. The emotive sensitivity expressed on the wrinkled forehead, in the mouth opened in the final breath, and in the intense, suffering glance of Goliath, is also felt in the flesh of the torso and the expression on the face of David.

The brown trousers and torn shirt which he is wearing contain passages of great pictorial synthesis, involving the use of long, separate brushstrokes and the juxtaposition, in the case of the shirt, of pure whites and greys, in a subtle play of transparency. Caravaggio used his own self-portrait for the head of Goliath, while in the David the features of his «little Caravaggio» are reproduced. A recent hypothesis suggests that the David is a youthful portrait of the artist, which would make the painting a double self-portrait. With conflicting feelings of disgust and pity, with one hand David brandishes his sword, on whose blade are letters which are not easy to decipher, but which may form the motto «Humilitas Occidit Superbiam»; the biblical hero is in fact a model of virtue. If one accepts the hypothesis that Scipione Borghese had commissioned Caravaggio for the work, it probably belongs to the last Roman period and would therefore be from before 1606. However, some scholars attribute the simplification of forms, the essential quality of the composition and the rapid application of brushstrokes to a later period.

In this case the painting may be interpreted as a gift, sent by the artist to Cardinal Scipione Borghese in the expectation of being granted grace, as the last attempt at drawing attention to the desperation of his circumstances and his wish to return to Rome.

GIAN LORENZO BERNINI, *APOLLO AND DAPHNE*
GALLERIA BORGHESE

In this case, the theme of metamorphosis provides the inspiration for a scene in which the vitality, movement and elegance particular to the baroque aesthetic exist side by side, finding their maximum expression. Bernini focuses his attention on the instant in which the nymph Daphne is transformed into a bay tree, the same instant in which the god Apollo succeeds in catching her up and seizing her. The impetus will be frozen in the most absolute immobility in a few seconds, but Bernini manages to make us feel the last palpitating instant of life in all its painful intensity, the extreme sensation of vitality of that fleeting moment which is inherent in the very dynamics of existence. The commission of the group is dated at the beginning of 1622, when the *Rape of Proserpine* was finished, and also came from Scipione Borghese. The prototypes for the figure of Daphne are to be found in the Maenads, in the bas-reliefs on antique sarcophagi. Bernini's profound knowledge of the antique is also evident in the figure of Apollo, based on the *Apollo Belvedere* in the Vatican Museums, from which, showing a precise philological knowledge of the antique, he even copies the footwear. In this case as well, the artist's aim is to represent several time sequences in a single image. With perfect stage direction he plans the placing of the group in exactly the right place in relation to the observer: on entering the room from the left we first notice Apollo's glance and the unexpected movement towards the nymph, then, standing in front, we become aware of the details of the metamorphosis, which the artist renders with matchless virtuosity.

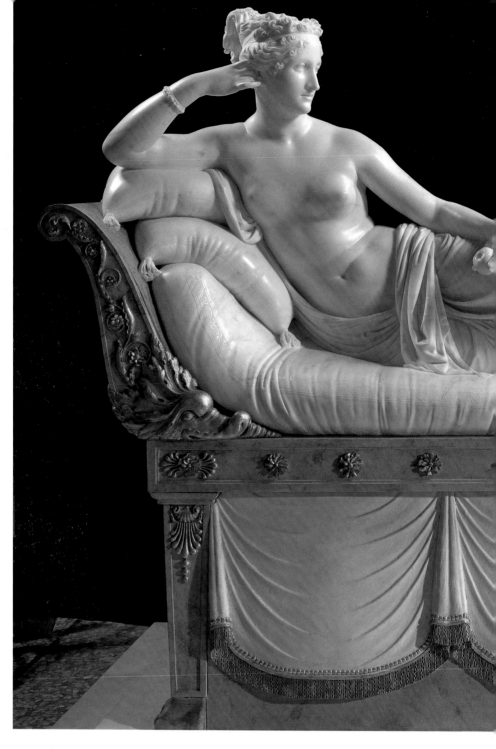

ANTONIO CANOVA, *PAULINE BORGHESE*
GALLERIA BORGHESE

The Napoleonic age marked the climax of Canova's international fame; the busts and statue portraits of members of Napoleon's family, including the famous portrait of *Pauline Borghese Bonaparte as Venus Victrix* belong to this period. In her left hand, Napoleon's sister holds the golden apple by which her beauty had been recognised by Paris to be superior to that of two other goddesses, Juno and Minerva.

The device of placing portrait heads on the idealised bodies of divinities or heroes was commonplace in Imperial Roman art, but the nude portrait of a person of rank was highly unusual at that time. Canova was effecting a metamorphosis of a historical person into an antique divinity. The work aroused great admiration among contemporaries; its subtle sensuality perfectly embodied the ideal of grace in the theory of Winckelmann «pleasure through reason».
This is another reason why the marble portrait of Pauline, with its extremely smooth forms, was

considered the apex of the neo-classical style. Antonio Canova had begun to prepare the work in 1804. We know that when it was exhibited in the artist's studio in 1808, the same year in which Camillo Borghese, the patron of the work and Pauline's husband, completed the payment, it was much visited and admired.

The Borghese prince took the work to Turin and it stayed there until, after the separation from Pauline and the fall of Napoleon, Camillo brought it back to Rome and displayed it in the family palazzo, where the sculpture was also on display at night, lit up by torches.

In this work, the exquisite softness of the modelling and the rapport with antique sarcophagi and Titian's Venus blend to form a perfect balance of «ideal beauty» and «natural beauty».

The marble is supported on the wooden structure of the bed. This conceals a mechanism, used at the time and recently restored, which enables the statue to be turned on its own axis, inverting the role between the work and the spectator: it is the sculpture which moves, while the observer is impressed by the fleeting images of perfect beauty.

MUSEO NAZIONALE ETRUSCO DI VILLA GIULIA

The museum was set up in 1889 to house the finds from outside of Rome in the national museum of Rome (*Museo Nazionale Romano*). It was housed, from its foundation, in the splendid villa built for pope Julius III (1550-1555) on via Flaminia. The original nucleus of findings from the *Falerii Veteres* site expanded with the addition of materials from the excavations in Latium and Umbria and from private collections, which led to an expansion of the building. When the Superintendence of Southern Etruscan Antiquities was established in 1939 the museum became autonomous. The current layout is the outcome of a scholarly reorganization begun in 1995 and not yet completed. The museum houses masterpieces of Etruscan art and many artisan artifacts that illustrate the most significant phases of the history of Etruscan culture, from the Villanova period (ninth to eighth centuries BC) to absorption of Roman culture (third to second centuries BC). The visitor's itinerary begins on the ground floor of the villa where the rooms are organized by geography, dedicated to Vulci (bronze cinerary urn in the form of a Villanova hut and the nenfro stone sculptures of the fourth century BC), Bisenzio (ceremonial cart and bronze situla with applied figurines of the Villanova period), Veio (acroterial statues from the temple at Portonaccio, including the famous *Apollo*), Cerveteri (splendid *Sarcophagus of a Married Couple*, bucchero ceramic vases and decorated

ceramics). The itinerary continues on the first floor with the *Antiquarium* exhibit, ordered by the types of materials in the collection, such as that of Augusto Castellani (tomb furnishings from the Castellani tomb at Palestrina from the Orientalizing era, fine ceramics, bronzes and magnificent gold finery); the rooms dedicated to the Pyrgi sanctuary (three gold sheets engraved in Etruscan and Phoenician, ceramic high-relief from the fifth century BC), now again open to the public after a period of restoration; recently organized sections focused on Etruscan inscriptions, the history of Villa Giulia and the museum, and the exquisite Attic goblet signed by Euphronios and Onesimos, from the sanctuary of Hercules at Cerveteri. These are followed, returning to the first storey, by the sections dedicated to Falerii and Capena (splendid terracottas from Falerii, including the *Apollo dello Scasato*), other Etruscan towns in ancient Latium (with the rich tomb furnishings from the Bernardini and Barberini tombs of the Orientalizing era and the so-called *Ficoroni cist* dated to the fourth century BC, from Palestrina) and in Umbria.

Above: *Head of Hermes*

Left: *Chigi Vase*   Facing page: *Apollo of Veio*

SARCOPHAGUS OF A MARRIED COUPLE

MUSEO NAZIONALE ETRUSCO
DI VILLA GIULIA

The terracotta sarcophagus, which was originally painted all over, comes from the necropolis of Banditaccia in Cerveteri and represents one of the masterpieces of clay sculpture from the end of the sixth century BC (circa 520 BC). It is actually a large urn for the ashes of the deceased, portraying a married couple reclining on the cushions of the banqueting bed (the *kline*), with its decorated feet and high mattress. The man, with his broad naked chest, tenderly embraces the shoulders of his elegantly dressed wife. In their hands, the couple must have held objects or foods for the banquet, one of the principal social events for the aristocratic classes, in which, in the Etruscan world, women could participate. The influence of ionic style is evident in the broad soft surfaces of the bodies, the lower parts of which are less defined, wrapped in the folds of the garment, in the focus on decorative details, and in the style of the elongated faces with convex foreheads, the almond-shaped eyes, the thin noses, protruding chins and typical archaic smiles. Worth noting is the attempt at rendering drapery between the two cushions.

GALLERIA NAZIONALE DI ARTE MODERNA

The National Gallery of Modern Art (Galleria Nazionale di Arte Moderna) is situated in the *Belle Arti* palace built by Cesare Bazzani in Valle Giulia between 1908 and 1911, on the occasion of the International Exposition. Between 1933 and 1934 the building was enlarged at the rear and a new expansion has been underway since 2004. It houses important collections of painting, sculpture and graphics by artists of the 19th and 20th centuries, principally Italians.
After the first thirty years, the collections were moved from the palace of the Exposition to its current seat, and the exhibition was laid out by regional schools.
The great season of the gallery was inaugurated under the direction of Palma Bucarelli, from the post-war years up to 1975, during which time a number of important exhibitions were held and important acquisitions were made (Piet Mondrian, Jackson Pollock, Alberto Burri, Lucio Fontana, Piero Manzoni). Recent acquisitions of home-museums such as that of Mario Praz in via Zanardelli, which houses the 19th-century furnishings and works of art collected by the well-known Roman anglist, critic and writer, and the Atelier-Museum of Hendrick Christian Andersen, a Danish sculptor active in Rome during the early 20th century, who also designed the elegant neo-15th century building in via Mancini which houses his sculptures, paintings and graphical works.
At the end of 1997 some new spaces were identified at the seat for the collections and

Vittorio Matteo Corcos,
Dreams

contemporary artistic events. In this area, previously occupied by former military barracks along via Reni, Iranian architect Zaha M. Hadid's project is under construction and will become the site of exhibition events and location for the collections during the 21st century. At this time the collections exhibited in the main museum seat in Valle Giulia are divided into four sectors: in the two southern wings that form part of the 1911 building, the original decorative structures have been recovered and works of the 19th century have been on display since June 1997.

The two northern wings, that date to the expansion of 1933, house works of the 20th century.

The itinerary through the south-west wing of the complex, dedicated to works of the 19th century, is organized by regional schools and includes neo-classical and romantic paintings and sculptures by the principal artists of Tuscany, Lombardy, Naples and Piedmont.

In addition to works of the Roman school of the early and late 20th century, there are also paintings by Italian artists who lived in Paris, such as Boldini, De Nittis and Zandomeneghi. These are followed by the most recent acquisitions of some important examples of French and Dutch painting, and a large group of pointillist paintings by Previati and Pellizza da Volpedo. The principal movements of the 20th century are also represented in the Gallery collection. Cezanne's last work, *Le cabanon de Jourdan* of 1906, came from the Jucker collection.

The itinerary continues through European informalism and American abstract expressionism, post-informalism, kinetic art, the principal figurative trends of pop art, up to *arte povera* and conceptual art that lead the way to future developments, as foreseen by the new expansion of the museum.

Above: Silvestro Lega,
The visit

Facing page: Gustav Klimt,
Three ages of woman

CATACOMB OF SAN SEBASTIANO

The church of San Sebastiano, once *basilica apostolorum*, stands on the righ-hand side of the Appian Way, about two kilometers from the Porta San Sebastiano. In ancient times this spot was a deep hollow, used as a pozzolana stone quarry and dubbed *ad catacumbus*, a term which in modern times has come to be a synonym for «underground cemetery».

The catacomb of Saint Sebastian originated in the galleries of the abandoned pit probably as early as the first century, and was developed towards the north and east mainly during the third century. The oldest building in the area was a villa constructed during the first century, to the west of the pit. It had a nearly square plan, and the rooms were arranged on two stories around a central courtyard.

Another similar, but later, edifice found under the basilica, the so-called *Villa Piccola*, contains geometric decorations characteristic of the wall painting of the time.

Along the north wall of the first villa and beyond it, at the edge of the hollow, were a series of mausoleums also from the first century. They lined the sides of a small street in a double file. Towards the middle of the second century, the bottom of the hollow was earthed over to create a small level open space, about 9 meters below the present church floor. On one side of it three mausoleums were built in succession. Shortly before 260 – perhaps in 258 – the clearing was covered with enough earth to raise the ground level by about 6 meters. On this new open area the *memoria* of Saint Peter and Saint Paul was built, bounded on the north by the row of first-century mausoleums, and on the west by the villa. The eastern loggia, known as the *triclia*, was raised 1.15 meters above the courtyard pavement. Its walls were painted with flowers, birds and animals, but there is barely a trace of them left today. Instead, numerous graffiti have been found with invocations to the Apostles, Peter and Paul. In the northwest corner of the courtyard stood the supposed *cella memoriae*. The Early Christian basilica differed enormously from the presentday church, which acquired its new appearance during the 17th century. It was built during the first half of the fourth century on the area comprising the *memoria* and the preexisting necropolis. Perhaps it was begun under Maxentius.

If so, it would be the prototype for the Constantinian basilicas of Sant'Agnese, San Lorenzo and Santi Marcellino e Pietro. It had the same east-west axis as the *memoria* and consisted of a central nave, flanked by two small side aisles joined by an ambulatory in the apse, to the west, and at the entrance, to the east. The U-shape of the whole resembled that of a circus.

A crypt was built, probably during the papacy of Damasus I (366-384), with a central altar that stood on a tomb, believed to be that of Saint Sebastian.

Outstanding among the numerous mausoleums lining the southern flank of the basilica and all erected in the fourth century is the rotunda of the Uranii (about 349).

CATACOMB OF SAINT CALLIXTUS

According to the sources, the catacomb of Saint Callixtus (Via Appia Antica, 102) is the oldest official cemetery of the Christian community of Rome. The complex was named after the deacon Callixtus, who was appointed head of the cemetery under Pope Zephyrinus (199-217) and who, when he was himself pope (217-22), enlarged it greatly. No less than nine third-century popes were buried here, in a crypt whose name reflects the fact. At certain points the cemetery complex is developed on as many as five levels, and its galleries spread over a distance of more than ten kilometres. The oldest part, situated to the right of the Appian Way as you leave Rome, presents two second-century independent galleries. The catacomb of Saint Callixtus, like the other catacombs, lay forgotten for a long while; the memory of where it stood was lost soon after the relics of the martyrs had been transferred to churches within the city and the Appia Ardeatina *memoria* removed to Saint Sebastian's – the one place that people continued to visit. The rooms of the crypts of Lucina had been known since the 18th century but it was Giovanni Battista De Rossi who discovered the burial site of pope Cornelius (251-53) in 1852, and then went

on to discover the crypt of the popes in 1854 and Severus' chamber. The Crypt of the Popes contains the tombs of nine Pontiffs who reigned between 230 and 283. At the moment the plan of the crypt is rectangular. A skylight provides illumination, and loculi and niches for sarcophagi line the side walls; it is probably an adaptment of a double chamber. However the original layout is now lost due to the final phases of the work and the significant restoration carried out during the 19th century by De Rossi. Opposite Deacon Severus' cubiculum is the cubiculum of the five saints with a wall painting showing six figures in a garden full of flowers, their arms outstretched in the typical attitude of prayer. Each figure has his name inscribed at his side with the greeting, «in peace».

The painting may be dated from the beginning of the fourth century, and in it the so-called compendium technique was used for the figures, each one taking shape with only a few, essential strokes of the brush. One of the oldest nuclei of the Saint Callixtus cemetery complex is the crypt of Lucina: the painting decorating the crypt shows the Good Shepherd, an allusion to Christ; it is an early third-century work, executed with a very rapid compendium technique.

CATACOMBS OF DOMITILLA

The subsoil of the city of Rome is mainly tufaceous rock, which is very crumbly and easy to excavate, and full of underground tunnels which from antique times had been created for various purposes (hydraulic connections, tufa quarries, crypto-porticos of villas and burials). The Christians in Rome found these galleries the simplest solution for burials, which needed more space than the cremation traditionally used by the Romans up to the second century AD. According to an unfounded tradition, the catacombs, the Christian underground cemeteries, were supposed to have originated as a refuge from persecution. The immense network of catacomb galleries created space for thousands of tombs distributed in the walls and on the ground; the richest tomb was the arcosolium type, where the cavity was dug out of the tufa, closed with a slab and surmounted by an arch, which was usually decorated with frescoes. On the walls there were loculi, closed with tiles or marble and ornamented with permanently lit oil lamps. They only occasionally bore the name of the deceased. The catacombs were used as cemeteries up to the fifth century; they then became sanctuaries for martyrs, visited by pilgrims from all over Europe. From the ninth century, the relics of saints began to be moved from the primitive tombs to churches within the walls of the city. Gradually the entrances to the underground cemeteries disappeared and the catacombs were forgotten about and stayed undiscovered until the 16th century, when Antonio Bosio initiated a systematic research.

The catacomb of Domitilla, whose entrance is situated between Piazza dei Navigatori and the first part of Via Ardeatina, is one of the major underground cemeteries of Rome and

was structured on top of pre-existing burial grounds. The land in this area belonged to Flavia Domitilla, niece of the consul, a noble Roman lady who was related to the Emperor Vespasian. Because of her Christianity, the Emperor banished her to exile in the Island of Ponza, where after a long martyrdom she eventually died.

SAN PAOLO FUORI LE MURA

The basilica of San Paolo fuori le Mura (Saint Paul's outside the Walls) stands on Via Ostiense, two kilometers from the Aurelian Walls and the Porta San Paolo. The present edifice is a reconstruction (1825-54) of the building destroyed in the fire of 1823. It has maintained the design, the dimensions and, in part, the surviving structures of the older church. The quadriporticus on its west front was built *ex novo* between 1890 and 1928.

In pre-Theodosian times, perhaps under Constantine, there was another small basilica on this site, built over a first or second century monument, which was the tomb and commemorative monument of the apostle Paul. The ruins of the apse, brought to light during the excavations of 1850, show that its orientation was the reverse of that of the present church. In 384, or perhaps 386, on the same site, the three reigning emperors, Theodosius I, Valentinian II and Arcadius began the construction of a new, large basilica, which was finished under Honorius in 395. The new basilica was created to give the tomb of Saint Paul a monumental setting, as had been done in Constantinian times with the basilica of Saint Peter which was, in many ways, its prototype. In front of the edifice on Via Ostiense was a large porticoed courtyard. Inside, five aisles separated by columns with connecting arches led to the transept, which was continuous, as in Saint Peter's, and slightly

projecting beyond the outer walls of the side aisles. The apse to its east was stately, wide as the central nave. The *cella memoriae* erected on the sepulchre of Saint Paul was not located on the chord of the apse, as was its twin in Saint Peter's, but on a spot quite close to the central nave. The column shafts were plundered from other buildings, but the capitals were specially prepared, composite in the central nave, Corinthian in the side aisles. The dimensions of the basilica were magnificent, surpassing those of all the other basilicas of its time. The breadth of the central nave was 24.22 meters, its length 89.87 meters and its height 30.77 meters. The inner side aisles were 8.96 meters wide and 16.22 meters high, the outer ones, 8.88 meters and 11.65 meters. The depth of

the transept was 24.20 meters, its width 71.01, and its height 26.81. The atrium was 66.80 meters wide and 59.08 meters long. Twenty-one windows flooded light upon the central nave, and the transept was illuminated by twelve arch windows and twelve round ones – but the apse and side aisles had no outside openings.

Not much is known of the original mosaic decoration of the basilica, which was completely redecorated with stucco and frescoes under Leo I (440-61). More important work was done under Gregory I (590-604), who raised the transept level by 90 centimeters and created a new setting for the tomb of Saint Paul, building above it, among other things, the principal altar of the basilica. The addition of a baptistery is attributable to Pope Symmachus.

CONTEMPORARY ARCHITECTURE

In recent years the important events held in Rome, from the world soccer championship in 1990 to the Jubilee in 2000 have been accompanied by architectural events of great influence and impact: the restructuring, expansion and new covering of the Olympic Stadium, the reinforcement of infrastructures, restoration in the historical center and, in general, the enhancement of the artistic and architectural heritage of the city with the restoration of villas, churches and the opening of new museums and exposition structures. In addition, leading contemporary architects have been called on to leave their imprint on the urban fabric of the city and Rome has also intended to become a site on the global circuit distinguished by the works of great international architects: in 1994 Renzo Piano won the competition for the new *Auditorium*, destined to become a new landmark of the urban landscape; in the outlying area of Tor Tre Teste, the American architect Richard Meier designed the church of the Jubilee *Dives Misericordioso*; Meier was also commissioned to design the new *Ara Pacis* museum complex, inaugurated with some controversy in 2005. At the end of the 1990's new international competitions were published for important projects: Iranian architect Zaha Hadid won the competition for the Center for Contemporary Arts, currently being constructed on the site formerly occupied by the Montello barracks on via Guido Reni; Massimiliano Fuksas won the competition for the new Congress Center in the Eur area known as *Nuvola*. The progressive expansion of the city into the surrounding countryside, the renovation of the hinterlands, conservation of green areas, the necessities

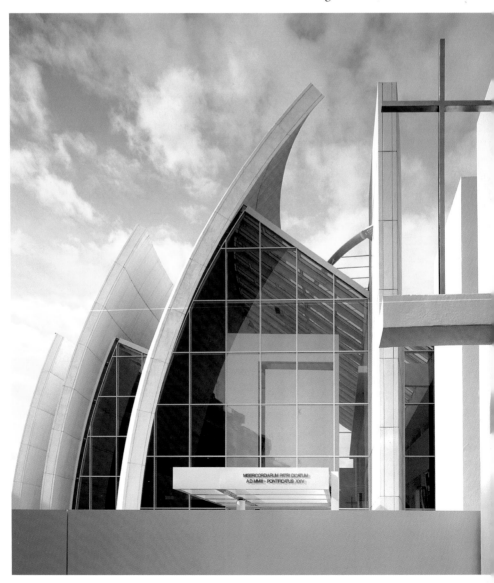

for mobility and transport: these are the most urgent themes being faced by the city today. Finally, the city must attempt to reconcile, as well as possible, the historical density of the city with contemporary experimentation. New forms must succeed in a dialogue with the culture of millenniums, through the urban, architectural and artistic stratifications that are the unique and distinctive characteristics of Rome.

Left: Richard Meier,
Dives Misericordioso

Above: Renzo Piano,
Auditorium

© 2008 SCALA GROUP S.p.A., Florence
All rights reserved
Translation: Jane Waller, Johanna Kreiner
Maps: © E-ducation.it

Photos:
© 2008 PHOTO SCALA, Florence
Except pages: 8, 12, 18, 19, 113: Foto Scala,
Firenze / Luciano Romano; p. 50: © ADP - su
Licenza Fratelli Alinari; pp. 74, 75: © Araldo de
Luca / CORBIS; p. 91: © The Bridgeman Art Library
/ Archivi Alinari, Firenze; pp. 100, 101, 102,
103, 104: © Musei Vaticani; p. 126: © Bildarchiv
Monheim / Archivi Alinari, Firenze

Printed by: Grafiche Flaminia, Foligno, 2008